P9-DUI-217

HANDBOOK
FOR THE
BEGINNING
MUSIC TEACHER

HANDBOOK FOR THE BEGINNING MUSIC TEACHER

Colleen M. Conway
University of Michigan

Thomas M. Hodgman
Adrian College

GIA Publications
Chicago

Cover art, book layout and design: Martha Chlipala

G-6625
ISBN: 1-57999-525-X

Copyright © 2006 GIA Publications, Inc.

GIA Publications, Inc.
7404 South Mason Avenue, Chicago 60638
www.giamusic.com

All rights reserved.
Printed in the United States of America

Contents

Part One: Fieldwork as an Undergraduate Student

Part Two: Student Teaching in Music

Preface

Handbook for the Beginning Music Teacher is a practical field experience guide and text for preservice (teacher education students) and beginning music teachers, P–12 (preschool through grade 12). Part One is designed to assist the undergraduate music education student as he or she navigates early observations and field experiences. Part Two is designed to assist music student teachers, and Part Three is geared toward the beginning music teacher.

The three sections of the book include sixteen real life stories written by beginning teachers. The names of children, other teachers, administrators, and schools have been changed to protect identity. Most stories include Questions for Discussion developed by the story authors.

Other features include two worksheets for preservice teacher reflection in Chapter One; fifteen protocols for doing observation in various music classrooms in Chapter Three; sample reflection worksheets for the student teacher, sample supervisor observation forms, and sample tools for collecting feedback from students in Chapter Six; research-based case studies for discussion in Chapter Seven; a music education job search database in Chapter Eight; a guide for use with a mentor in Chapter Eleven; and a professional development checklist for the beginning music teacher in Chapter Twelve. Each of the three parts of the book also features a reference list with relevant research and suggestions for further reading. The Epilogue includes five stories written by beginning teachers in response to the question "What keeps you going?"

How to Use This Book

If you are an undergraduate student who is just beginning observations in schools, you will find the material in Part One of the book to be most helpful in the work you are doing right now. You can look ahead to Parts Two and Three of the book on student teaching and the first years of teaching for further preparation.

If you are currently student teaching or preparing for student teaching, you may still find the material in Part One of the book useful. The early teaching experiences worksheet in Chapter One works well for the early days of student teaching, and the stories from preservice teachers will resonate with student teaching experiences as well. The observation tools found in Chapter Three should be useful for student teachers because it is recommended that some time during student teaching be spent observing music classrooms as well as teaching.

If you are a first- or second-year teacher and have already completed preservice fieldwork and student teaching, you will find the information in Part Three regarding mentoring and induction to be timely. You may find that the information provided in Parts One and Two of the book serves as a reminder of what good music classrooms look like and provides you with models to strive for in your first year. Wherever you are on the continuum of becoming a music teacher, we hope you will find this book helpful in your growth. We encourage you to stick with it and hope that the stories in the "What Keeps Them Going?" section in the Epilogue will serve as motivators for the tough times.

Acknowledgments

We would like to acknowledge many of the contributors to various sections and tools in the book including:

- University of Michigan undergraduate students Kate Bowerman, Lauren Peterson, Jessica Schmeck, and Michael Swain.

- University of Michigan graduate students Derek Bannasch, Ryan Hourigan, and Jill Reese.

- University of Michigan graduates Daniel Albert, Jamal Duncan, Armand Hall, Corynn Nordstrum, Stephanie Perry, Andrew Schulz, Diane Strasser Platte, Brittany Uschold, and Adam Warshafsky.

- Michigan music teachers Erin Hansen and Regina White Herring.

- Music education colleagues Louis Bergonzi, Suzanne Burton, Robert Erbes, Herbert Marshall, and Debbie Lynn Wolf.

Part One:

Fieldwork as an Undergraduate Student

Chapter One
Developing as a Music Teacher

Growth as a Musician and a Teacher

You have entered into music teacher education at a very exciting time. The broad field of music education in recent years has made the recruitment and retention of music teachers a major priority. The Music Educators National Conference (MENC), the national professional organization for music teachers, has had your interests at the top of its national agenda since 2002. They continue to work hard to provide instruction and support for preservice and in-service music teachers. The National Association of Schools of Music (NASM), the prime accrediting body for undergraduate music education programs, has been actively working to improve the preparation of music teachers as well. Professors in your music teacher education department have no doubt been involved in recent discussions and meetings regarding the preparation of music teachers for the classrooms of the future.

Music teacher educators have come to some agreement regarding the preparation of future music teachers, and this preparation begins across the board with the development of musicianship. Music education students are required to study applied lessons on instruments or voice, perform in a variety of ensembles, develop their aural skills and music notation abilities, study music history and world music, and gain skills at the piano and in conducting. What is challenging for you as the music education student is balancing this sequential development of personal musicianship skills with the development of skills needed to teach these same concepts to children of various ages and in various musical contexts.

Music educators agree that strong musicians make strong music teachers. It is not possible to be a good music teacher if you are not also a good musician. This first section of the *Handbook for Beginning Music Teachers* is designed to help the undergraduate music education student gain the necessary skills and attitudes needed for success as a music teacher. It focuses on the early experiences that the undergraduate may have in school settings and suggests ways of thinking about music teaching and learning that the student must consider.

This first story highlights the importance of strong musicianship in the growth of a teacher.

Musicianship Carries the Way

Last fall I took a course on Elementary Instrumental Methods (i.e., how to teach beginning band). In addition to the weekly lectures, we had a fieldwork component at a nearby elementary school. I arrived on the first day of fieldwork terrified at what I was about to experience. I was informed that I was to be working with beginning clarinetists, and it had been several years since I had taken clarinet methods.

Though I'd had experience with beginning bassoonists (bassoon is my primary instrument), the clarinetists presented a whole set of challenges I wasn't really prepared for. In the few minutes before class began, I put my clarinet, on loan from the university, together and desperately tried to remember a few key fingerings and how to form an embouchure. I was barely able to piece together "Hot Cross Buns" in B-flat concert before the three little clarinetists walked into the room.

The first few minutes, needless to say, were pretty bad. I tried to explain the mechanics of how to breathe and how to sit and hold the instrument. As a result I talked and talked and talked. Sensing the students' boredom, I moved the activity to playing. I modeled "Hot Cross Buns" for them, and they responded in turn. Fortunately, the kids enjoyed playing the clarinet, and as long as I kept the activities to musical ones, the lessons were much more productive.

Over the course of the following weeks, I came to realize that even though I am not a master clarinetist and probably never will be, I am a good musician. If I use my musicianship and the strength of my personality in my teaching, they can help make up for the lack of knowledge I have about the particular instrument. As I learned more in my methods courses, I chose activities that would improve my musicianship and allow me the chance to use my strengths. Thus, my fieldwork students and I would sing tunes and bass lines by rote before we'd play them. We'd engage in movement activities designed to help teach both a steady beat and subdivision. The students seemed to enjoy these activities, and their ability to play their tunes on the clarinet improved (I hope) because of the singing and moving. My confidence as a teacher increased as well.

As time progressed, of course, I learned more about the idiosyncrasies of the individual instruments. This is invaluable to the instrumental teacher. But looking back on that first fieldwork experience, I would say that the greatest lesson I learned is that the most important thing a music teacher brings to the experience is the strength of his or her own musicianship.

–Derek Bannasch

Questions for Discussion

- How secure are you in your own musicianship? What areas (tonal or rhythmic) would you like to improve?
- What types of activities can you suggest for teaching students on an instrument or in a course with which you lack familiarity?
- Discuss the link between competence on your major instrument to being a successful music educator. How do these skills transfer to the classroom?

View of the Music Classroom from a Teacher's Perspective

One of the first steps beginning music teachers must take in their development is to recognize where they have come from and what effect that has on their beliefs regarding what it means to be a music teacher. Consider that your own memory of "music class" from elementary, middle, or high school is a memory of you as a student, and the perspective of the teacher in these settings may be very different. Early on in the undergraduate degree, the music education student must try to view the music classroom from the teacher's perspective rather than from that of a student. Writing autobiographies or examining personal stories of teaching may help in this transition. It is also critical to observe music teaching and learning in a variety of classroom settings, including early childhood, elementary general, band, choral, strings, and less traditional settings. A large majority of states have P–12 music certification, so music teachers need to prepare to teach in all types of classrooms. The story below from a preservice music teacher discusses her growth during fieldwork in learning to view the music classroom from a broader perspective.

I Don't Think We're in Kansas Anymore

The morning of my first fieldwork assignment I woke up with a feeling of nervous excitement and thought, "Finally, a break from all the music theory, musicology, and natural science distribution requirements for a chance to do what I actually signed up for in my major: teaching music to real live kids!" At 6:45 a.m., I met up with three other peers from my methods class, and we carpooled to our assigned school. On the way we discussed our lesson plans, our anxieties about having to model secondary instruments, and whether we thought we would actually be able to wake up and function at such an early hour every day for the rest of our careers. Ultimately, we all came to the conclusion that we were completely clueless as to what was in store.

The morning went by so quickly it felt like it was over before it had started. Reflecting back on that morning, the biggest surprise was the fact that the beginning band program I had walked into only faintly resembled the beginning band program I was expecting: the one I was most familiar with, the one I thought all programs looked like, the one from my hometown. I don't know what I was thinking! This band class was held on folding chairs in the gym with one teacher trying to educate a sea of fifth graders. Even though they had been in band for about two weeks, a handful of clarinet players in this band were assembling their instruments backwards.

Coming to the realization that all music education programs across the country did not resemble the familiar setting I had grown up in was a real adjustment for me. I had attended a large, wealthy suburban school district known for its excellent schools. Music education in my hometown was well supported, especially financially, and the state I was from had a music education association that organized all the festivals and competitions on a statewide level. In my middle school, beginning band started in the sixth grade. We had three directors, two rehearsal spaces, and three different ensembles. My high school band program had a band faculty comprised of two directors, three percussion specialists, one drill writer, two color guard instructors, and a slew of private lesson teachers. When I started my fieldwork only two years out of high school, I naively assumed all music education programs were set up that way.

In addition to that struggle was the bit of loyalty I felt toward music education in my hometown and state. Again, only two years out of high school, I still looked back upon my experiences in middle school and high school band very fondly. There were a lot of memories and friendships I took away from my band experiences, and I had yet to take on the mindset of perceiving and analyzing my old band programs from the perspective of the future music educator I was becoming. Once I shifted from the mindset of band student to that of a music educator, I was able to be more critical and objective about my hometown band programs and even the methods and techniques the band directors used.

As an out-of-state music major, I immediately became exposed to a whole new state's music education program. I was unfamiliar with the state organization acronyms, didn't know the procedures or rules for any of the festivals, and felt pretty in the dark.

As fieldwork went on and my methods classes got more and more involved, it became easier for me to perceive music education programs from all sorts of perspectives. I realized that while "there's no place like home," a typical music education program simply does not exist. So I set out to learn all kinds of perspectives, procedures, and methods that would one day come together and become *my* music education program.

—Jessica Schmeck

Questions for Discussion

- Do you have any preconceived expectations of your assigned fieldwork setting?
- What memories from your own experiences in music affect your views of the field?
- What aspects of your personal experience might you adopt?
- What aspects of your personal experience might you choose NOT to adopt?

Making the Connection between Theory and Practice

Music education students must constantly grapple with the potential differences between what is presented in music education courses and what actually happens in school music programs. Students must use what they are learning in music education courses to examine what we might call "teaching practice" on campus and in school observations. The observation tools in Chapter Three provide some language for making these connections.

The progressive music education student attends every on-campus rehearsal focused on issues of teaching and learning. While rehearsing in on-campus ensembles, music students should ask themselves: What is the conductor thinking? How is he or she modeling teaching methods discussed in music education methods classes? How are the goals of this ensemble the same or different from the goals for P–12 music? What are we learning today? What strategies seem to be working for this group of learners? Taking on this disposition of "teacher" should allow the music education student to quickly become more aware of important issues of music teaching and learning.

All music teachers must make on-the-spot decisions regarding students and music many times in every music class or rehearsal. Because every music class and rehearsal context is different, music teachers try to prepare future educators for whatever they might face in any context by providing them with the skills to make what we might call principled and insightful decisions about how to proceed in a classroom. Principled decisions are possible with an understanding of how children learn music and what constitute appropriate goals for school music students. Insightful decisions can be made if a novice teacher is able to consider not only his or her own personal experiences in music education but many other models as well (primarily other models observed or experienced in preservice fieldwork). The content of these principled and insightful decision-making areas constitutes what we refer to as the theory of teaching. However, actually learning how to put all of these ideas into practice with real students is always a challenge.

Striking a balance between gaining the knowledge of music teaching theories and working with real students in authentic teaching settings is difficult. We encourage undergraduates to reflect regularly on how their past experiences in school music or other musical organizations relate to material and new ideas being introduced in the undergraduate curriculum. This next story by undergraduate student Lauren Peterson presents her journey in junior-year fieldwork in elementary and secondary instrumental methods class and highlights the importance of having an open mind and a healthy attitude and disposition toward what happens in real music classrooms. She describes trying to teach in a classroom that did not welcome her ideas about teaching and writes about what can be learned from fieldwork that cannot be learned from a book or in a methods class.

Rule No. 1

When asking for advice from a well respected teacher in my community, I was told "Rule number one of early teaching is: you don't have an opinion for five years." What that was implied, I wasn't quite sure at the time. I discovered exactly what he meant as soon as I started my preservice teaching.

Walking into my preservice work (with fifth grade beginners in the fall and later with high school band in the winter term), my experience was much like that of any other student in the same position. I thought in much the same way I would think prior to any other objective test: "I can do this. This is what I have been going to school for. I know everything I need to know to get me through." The fact is that musically I did know everything I needed. I knew fingerings; I knew time signatures and rhythms; I knew intervals, solfege, and melodic material. And by the time the lesson was done, I thought I had done pretty well—if I had been teaching to a collegiate audience, that is. These kids didn't care about all my musical knowledge! They wanted to have fun and maybe learn something about music at the same time. My error was in my opinion of myself; by relying so much about my own knowledge and forgetting the students, my very first preservice teaching experiences looked more like an episode of Jeopardy than an engaging beginning band class.

By the time I reached high school, my opinion problem shifted from my overconfidence about (and inevitable overreliance on) my musicianship to overconfidence about the effectiveness of my lesson plans. You see, I had all these ideas: how to empower students to take on more responsibility for their playing, using guiding questions instead of giving commands, and tying personal performance into the musical context, etc. So I went onto the podium armed with my own musical knowledge, my score, and my lesson plan. I asked all the questions, talked about the composer's life and the musical context, and by the time I was done executing all my great ideas, I realized I had a problem. The problem wasn't in having these ideas, but in not realizing that my full-fledged teaching philosophy and style were neither what these students were used to, nor were they interested in how the composer's life influenced the music and how it should influence their performance. In spite of my lesson planning and my knowing "everything" I needed to know, these kids didn't want what I knew. They wanted what *they* knew. They wanted the learning environment that was most comfortable for them; they wanted to learn in the way to which they had grown accustomed. What I learned in my methods classes was not the way these students wanted to learn.

My point is this: having opinions about your teaching can lead you to expect things that are likely not there, just as I expected my musicianship and lesson ideas to be everything I needed in the classroom. Teaching isn't just about your expectations; it's about your reactions to your students and to your environment. Like it or not, part of the preservice experience is learning to fly by the seat of your pants because so much of what you do after you graduate will be about how well you can think on your feet. Having opinions and expectations will only hinder your ability to think fast. If you are able to go in with an open mind and let yourself think fast, you will learn much more about yourself and how to be the best music educator you can.

That being said, it is essential to take advantage of any observation prior to preservice teaching to get to know your audience (i.e., your student body) as much as possible. If you don't take the time to put your opinions aside (your knowledge and ability coming into the classroom, your own judgment of how successful you might be, etc.) and get to know what your students are all about, your teaching only becomes valuable to you, when your students are the ones who really count. Trying to force an established program to meet your needs is not an option, especially when one of the main purposes of preservice training is to make you more adaptable. Train yourself during your preservice training (that's what it's there for) to adapt to your students. This does not mean in any way, shape, or form to ignore your own needs as a preservice teacher. Make sure you are armed with as much knowledge as possible about the who, what, and how of your situation; that way you will be prepared for anything your students can and will shoot at you during the course of your service. Start doing this early, and you might come to the same conclusion I did: you learn a lot more from not having an opinion than from having one.

—Lauren Peterson

Questions for Discussion

- What does the author warn against?
- What exactly does Rule No. 1 mean? How can it be applied to your preservice experience?
- Does Rule No. 1 apply to all opinions or only some? If some, which kinds?

This chapter concludes with a School Observation Reflection Worksheet and a First Fieldwork Teaching Experiences Reflection Worksheet to provide a framework for discussion of personal views and biases. (Purchasers of this book for personal use may make photocopies.) More specific details regarding arranging the fieldwork can be found in Chapter Two, and more details regarding what to observe in music settings are in Chapter Three. The tools provided here are geared toward the relationship between past experience and the observation or fieldwork.

School Observation Reflection Worksheet

Questions to consider before the observation:

- What do you remember about your own experience of music in this type of setting?

- If you did not have music in a setting like this, what are your preconceived notions about music in this setting?

- What do you expect to see or hear?

- What would a good lesson look and sound like?

Questions to consider during the observation:

- What must have happened before today in order for this lesson to happen today?

- How does the teacher prioritize instruction? What is addressed first?

- What might I do if I were the teacher?

- What skills and attitudes does this teacher need to have a good lesson?

Questions to consider after the observation:

- What is my reaction to this experience?

- How does it relate or not relate to my past experiences?

First Fieldwork Teaching Experiences
Reflection Worksheet

Questions to consider before teaching in a fieldwork setting:

- What are my biggest concerns regarding teaching in this setting? Why?

- What is my personal goal for this teaching experience?

Questions to consider during the teaching:

- Am I demonstrating good musicianship?

- What is the reaction from the students? Am I aware of students' level of participation, focus, and interest? Am I responding to the students' needs?

- How is my pace? Am I moving too quickly? Too slowly?

Questions to consider after the teaching:

- What were my strengths during this lesson?

- What should I consider for my next experience?

- In what ways was I able to read the students? Did I respond to what I read?

- How do I prepare myself for the next experience?

Chapter Two
Early Fieldwork

In many music education programs students may be given a list of suggested music teachers to contact for arranging fieldwork. In some programs, the faculty will arrange the placement, but in other settings it may be up to the student to work out the logistics of the fieldwork placement. Most fieldwork begins with some sort of observation. In some instances the fieldwork component may include only observation for a complete semester. In some undergraduate programs a student might do multiple observations of various music classroom settings while in others the same classroom may be observed multiple times. Some fieldwork includes teaching as well as observing. The student may be asked to interview teachers or P–12 students as part of a fieldwork requirement. The student should be sure to understand the expectations of the fieldwork before locating a placement. Know whether you are only to observe or whether you are to teach in some way and how many visits to the same classroom are required. Find out if you need to speak with the teacher before the visit, after the visit, or both. Know if you are expected to interact in some way with the students. Be clear regarding the assignments and the goals for the fieldwork.

When contacting the P–12 music teacher (often referred to as the co-operating or collaborating teacher) remember that they are very busy people. It may take the teacher a few days to return an e-mail or phone call. The student must plan for this. Try to give the teacher several days' notice if you are coming out to observe. Be sure to identify yourself in the e-mail, and make reference to the college or university professor who suggested you visit that school. Make the expectations of the fieldwork clear in this initial contact. If you need to interview the teacher or interact with the students, this may affect whether the teacher has time to accommodate you. If you are expected to teach as part of the fieldwork, the teacher must know this right from the beginning.

First Visit to the Schools

Once you receive a response from a music teacher suggesting that it is appropriate for you to visit on a certain day and time, be sure you have clear directions to the school. Your music education department may have a list of all the local schools and their mailing addresses. Try to find directions ahead of time so you are certain to know how to get to the school.

Even if you are just going to the school to observe, you should dress like a professional. Jeans, shorts, t-shirts, or sneakers are not appropriate. The earlier you begin to think and act like a "teacher," the easier the transition to real teaching will be. Be sure to give yourself extra time to find the school so that you arrive promptly. It often takes time to find parking at a school and check in at the office. Go to the office before trying to find the music room. Some schools require a visitor name badge. You may even have to return to your car with a parking sticker. Be sure to plan for this time.

If possible, arrive in the classroom approximately twenty minutes before the class begins so that you have an opportunity to chat with the co-operating teacher before the class you observe begins. Because you usually only have five to seven minutes between classes to talk to the co-operating teacher, try to ask important questions before class starts. Sometimes the teacher may be arriving from another school and will not be there until the start of the class. Find out these details from the co-operating teacher via e-mail or phone previous to the day of the visit.

What to Expect in an Observation

Chapter Three provides some specific criteria for observing a variety of music settings. One should expect that students in the courses might wonder who you are. If the co-operating music teacher does not introduce you to students, be prepared to introduce yourself. It is best to practice referring to yourself as Mr. or Ms. Take advantage of any opportunity you get to interact with the students. We suggest trying to participate in any musical activity in which the students are engaged. Check with the music teacher to make sure that this is appropriate. Bring your instrument if you are visiting an instrumental music classroom so you may play along with the students. Again, check with the music teacher to ask whether this is appropriate. Be sure that you know what you are looking for when you go to an observation. Also know what is expected of you in terms of documentation. You may need to take notes or collect information during the observation.

Types of Early Teaching Experiences

Beyond observation, the types of early teaching experiences vary a great deal. In elementary general music, the first experience may be to teach a new song to a group of elementary general music students (four or five minutes of instruction). Instrumental and secondary choral music students are often asked to conduct sectionals or small groups of students in their early fieldwork. Small groups provide you with the opportunity to get to know students more individually so that if you get in front of the larger ensemble or class later, you have already built relationships with some students in small groups. A disadvantage to sectionals and small groups is that the co-operating teacher is not usually in the room where you are teaching, so you may not get any feedback regarding your work.

Another early experience in the secondary setting may be to warm up the ensemble. Some early fieldwork students also have the opportunity to conduct a full ensemble or teach a complete lesson in general music. Music education students often struggle with planning for these early field experiences. It is sometimes difficult for the co-operating teacher to let you know what you will be doing the next time you visit because it often covers an entire week of instruction. It is hard for the co-operating teacher to predict what the students will need to focus on in a week. The music education student must be ready to jump in and try some things even if there was no time to plan. Be as proactive as you can with the co-operating teacher regarding what musical content will be covered the next time you visit, but know that some of what you have to do will be last minute. The story by Kate Bowerman at the end of this chapter addresses some of the issues of the "inauthentic nature" of the fieldwork experience. She suggests that although the logistics of fieldwork are often less than perfect, teacher growth can still occur.

Understanding Context

Whether you are observing or teaching, it is important to try to get a sense of where students may have been before you arrived and where they are heading after you leave. Try to speak for a few minutes with the co-operating teacher before the class begins. It is also important to pay special attention to other issues of context. Who are these students? What are their backgrounds? What challenges of music teaching are specific to this setting? What does this teacher do to enhance this setting? What could the teacher do differently? What would I do if this were my teaching position? The bottom line in observing and early fieldwork is to realize that what works in some settings will not work in all settings. Try to get a sense of contextual issues so you can make intelligent decisions regarding what about this teaching setting might transfer to a future setting and what might not. The protocols in Chapter Three include some of these contextual considerations.

Working with Other Music Education Student Colleagues

You may have the opportunity to attend a fieldwork visit with a colleague. There is value in the car ride to and from the observation or teaching experience. Make the most out of the opportunity to discuss the fieldwork experience with your colleagues. You can teach one another many things.

One of the most challenging aspects of learning to be a teacher is getting a sense of your own personal identity. This story from preservice teacher Michael Swain outlines his growth in this area.

I Am Mr. Swain

As an undergraduate student in music education, I had many learning experiences participating in observations and fieldwork. Through my observations, I realized that my perspectives on teaching and learning had greatly changed. I was able to be critical of certain methods that the teachers used, and I formed models in my mind of both good and bad ways to teach music. I began to get a realistic sense of the skills needed to be a successful music educator.

I was also fortunate enough to observe teachers with varying approaches to music education. I began to compare these real life scenarios with one another and with the ideas discussed in my university classes. I was forming a template of the ideal music teacher in my head, and it was constantly shaped by observing music teachers in action. After reflecting upon these observations, I got the chance to actually get in front of students and do some teaching of my own.

The first scenario as part of my music education fieldwork was to teach small groups of fifth grade woodwind players who had just recently started playing their instruments. It was comforting that I was also a beginning woodwind player, but I also felt slightly incompetent in front of my students. It became very clear that there was a gap between my theories of music education and putting those theories into action.

Before each lesson I planned an activity for the young musicians that aimed to increase their musical knowledge. I remember one lesson plan that involved the students and me singing the notes we had covered thus far on the instruments.

I tried to explain the importance of being able to hear the correct pitch and how singing could actually help their playing. I demonstrated the first five notes in a major scale, my voice shaky from nerves. When I asked the group to join me, I couldn't get anything more than a muffled half singing-half chanting reply. I had the students play the first note to get it in their minds and tried to get them to sing the correct pitch. After another atonal response, we shared a brief moment of awkward silence. My lesson plan had crumbled before my eyes, and I felt that I had failed.

Even if this lesson was carefully crafted and pedagogically sound, some other factors influenced my success with the students. Part of this had to do with my developing identity as a music teacher. My previous teaching experience was very informal, but in this case I was "Mr. Swain." My mind raced during the lessons. If the students seemed disengaged, I became worried about my abilities as a teacher and about the students' perceptions of my teaching. I was also attempting to do something completely new. I knew that the singing exercise was great for developing musicality, but I didn't know how the students would react to my attempts at getting them to try a method with which they were unfamiliar.

After reflecting on my teaching experiences with these fifth graders, I felt I was better prepared to be a music teacher. I got to experience the excitement of successfully teaching music skills to beginning instrumentalists on instruments completely different from my own. I realized that I saw more improvement in my students when I was confident in my musical abilities, focused on a specific task, and willing to be flexible. I also got a better idea of the demeanor I must exhibit when working with this specific age group. Teaching music is an active, complex process that calls for the teacher to be knowledgeable and able to change with the situation. As the weeks rolled by, I was able to detach myself from the lesson plan and teach in the moment. Although I only taught these kids for a short time each week, I learned a tremendous amount about myself as a future teacher.

–Michael Swain

Questions for Discussion

- What are some of your fears regarding your first teaching experience with real students?
- Do you think it was a good or bad idea for Michael to try something new with his students?
- What do you think he means when he says that he learned how to be himself with students of that age?

This final story in the chapter from undergraduate student Kate Bowerman describes her journey to find her identity as a teacher despite what she calls "the unrealistic nature" of the fieldwork classrooms.

Lost without a Pace

During my fieldwork experience, I found my biggest issue to be pacing. Although I knew the lesson sequence very well and had a good grasp of method, I didn't really know what to look for to determine the success of my students. I knew what my final product should be, but I didn't really know, on a short-term basis, if my teaching was effective. This led to pacing that was often too fast, but sometimes even too slow. I found this was not only because of my own inexperience, but also the unique problem of irregular interaction in preservice fieldwork.

I've finally developed an efficient practice procedure for myself in college, and my challenge now is to bring that knowledge to the classroom. It's easier to learn technique than it is to learn pacing, and unfortunately, in my experience with fieldwork, it was difficult to deal with this reality.

For my entire junior year I spent Thursday mornings at local schools practicing my craft in an (unfortunately) unrealistic situation. The professors and co-operating teachers try to make it as real as possible, but this can't happen in a once-a-week interaction with children. During the first semester, I was at an elementary school at 7:30 a.m. for half an hour with the same fifth grade beginning band every week. I started with small-group lessons (two or three children), moved on to larger sectionals, and only for the last two classes or so taught the whole band.

During the winter semester I went to a high school where they had block scheduling, and I often didn't know which band I'd be working with that day, the top wind ensemble or the lower concert band. After working with instrument sectionals for half the semester, I took the podium to rehearse the entire band.

At the elementary school I began with small group lessons for fifteen minutes at a time working on short melodic and rhythmic activities. I never really knew what was going on for the rest of the week, just that the children were learning to play their instruments mostly by a traditional method. When I got there, I knew I had very little time to work on musicality without instruments (sometimes with their horns). Sometimes I found the activity I had chosen was too difficult for my small group of students, and I felt like my only choice was to drop the activity and try something easier or leave it incomplete. This detracts from any sense of accomplishment that the children feel, making them less likely to want to come back to band the next day. I often wondered if some of them would drop band at the end of the year because they remembered an unsuccessful lesson they had with me. However, if I had them on a long-term basis it would be easier to choose a lesson plan. Seeing the same students every day, I'd choose an appropriate lesson plan, and I wouldn't feel trapped with one I arbitrarily came up with.

Later that same semester I got my chance to do an activity with the whole group. My classmate and I collaborated on one tune: "Jingle Bells." I taught some melodic and rhythmic patterns, and, afterwards, he taught the tune. While I was in front of them it was difficult for me to gauge the students' reactions because I was so concerned with examining myself. I didn't realize then that in fact paying more attention to the students would really tell me how well I was doing. Because during my own class periods I practiced these activities with my classmates, I was so used to my audience getting it right the first time around, and I didn't really know what to do when half of the elementary class didn't come anywhere near the right notes for my tonal patterns. Also, many of them couldn't feel a steady beat, so this made my rhythmic activities difficult. My professor told me more than once to "try that pattern again." If I had paid more attention to what was happening at that time in the classroom, I would've realized I was going too fast for most of the kids to follow. Coupled with my abnormally fast speaking voice (which I have worked very hard to slow down) I now see why the kids weren't getting it: I wasn't slow enough to give them the chance.

I found I had the opposite problem at the high school I worked at during second semester of my junior year. Toward the end of the term I took the podium to rehearse a medley of tunes from *Les Miserables*. I had had a week to look at this score, but I had only seen this band once before because of the block schedule. I knew which parts I wanted to rehearse and had a very detailed rehearsal plan, but I hadn't yet learned that it is most important (with high school bands) to keep them playing as much as possible for most of the period. In the tune I rehearsed, "At the End of the Day," there were many short solo lines and small-group entrances. Instead of nitpicking these portions, I should have had the group play more of the melody parts that appear later in the section. It would have kept them involved and kept the pace fast. I spent too much time with the three bassoons and two tubas trying to coordinate their not-so-significant entrance. I was critiqued later not only by my professor but by written comments from the students stating that this was the wrong idea. To keep the pace up in a high school band class, the teacher should rehearse large chunks of music more often than short pieces. The students were very well behaved and polite, thankfully. But now I know that I'll need to engage my own band for a long time with group activities before I get the engagement necessary for such detailed rehearsal.

Because the fieldwork situations are so unrealistic, it's easy to blame the school system for an unsuccessful lesson. Luckily, though, so many unsuccessful classes added up to many lessons learned for me. One of my first assignments in my classroom will be to set a pace and keep it and always look to the success of my students to determine my own efficacy.

–Kate Bowerman

Questions for Discussion

• Assuming you've taught private lessons or sectionals before, think about times when your student just wasn't getting it. How could you have changed your technique without losing pace or patience? How will these techniques help you in the classroom?

• You can't plan for every single mishap in a classroom. Think about some ways you can hold your students' attention even when they're frustrated and ready to quit.

Conclusion

Music education students involved in preservice observation and fieldwork must remember that it is very easy to criticize from the back of the room. Try in your observations to really consider what you might do if you were the teacher in the setting. As Kate mentioned, even in your fieldwork teaching it is sometimes easy to fault the school or the schedule or the logistics for lessons that do not go well.

Not all educational problems are easily solved. Work to see what priorities the co-operating teacher has made. Not everything can be fixed at once. What do they tackle first? How and why? If you are doing an observation for a class you will most likely need some sort of written reflection or description of the observation to hand in to your professor. Even if you are not observing for a course, it is useful to write down your observations and thoughts for further reflection after the visit. The observational tools in Chapter Three are designed to facilitate this documentation of your observations. These tools are different from the reflection worksheets in Chapter One, as those were designed to connect your past experiences with the observations. After you have completed the observations and/or fieldwork, be sure to send a thank you note to the co-operating teacher for opening his or her classroom to you.

Chapter Three
Guides for Observation in a Music Setting

As suggested in Chapters One and Two, most music education programs include some freshman- and sophomore-level observations in a variety of music settings. The tools in this chapter are meant to guide your thinking as you observe teachers in various music classrooms. Each observation tool was developed by a music teacher with expertise in specific areas of music education. Each has a slightly different format, and we would encourage you to mix and match the observation forms for use in your own work. You may also consider using these forms as a guide and developing your own observation protocol more specific to the setting being observed or the requirements of the fieldwork. It is suggested that you study the observation questions or tools before the observation. When you get to the classroom, try to spend as much time watching as possible. Then, immediately following the observation, take time to write your responses, evaluations, comments, and questions regarding what you saw.

The protocols may not be ideal for all fieldwork observations. In some cases you may return to observe the same setting again and may only document some of the issues on the observation protocols during any one visit. Or it may happen that you do not have enough content knowledge to address all the issues on the protocol. For example, on the string class protocols there are questions about bowing and bow style. If you have not had strings class in your degree program yet, you may not be able to address the string-specific items on the observation protocol. However, the protocol authors felt it important to include the content-specific information on the observation forms so that at the very least the beginning teacher will be aware that there are issues to note.

The first four protocols (Early Childhood Music, Elementary General Music, Beginning Band, and Elementary Choral Music) were developed by Herbert Marshall from the University of Michigan. He has taught early childhood music, elementary general music, elementary choral music, and beginning band in the public schools. In addition, his primary research area is early childhood and elementary general music education. Marshall also provided the protocol for

Non-Traditional Ensembles, as he has some experience with world music ensembles as well. He currently works with undergraduate music education students at the University of Michigan, and preparing those students for fieldwork observations is an important aspect of his work.

The Beginning Strings, Middle and High School Strings, and High School Full Orchestra protocols were developed by Erin Hansen. She is the Director of Orchestras at Saline High School in Saline, Michigan, where she directs the high school string and full orchestras in addition to working with beginning strings and a fiddling ensemble. Previous to her appointment at Saline High School, Erin worked with fifth through eighth grade string students at Saline Middle School and Heritage Elementary.

The Middle and High School General Music and Middle and High School Choral protocols were developed by Jill Wozniak Reese. She currently works with preschool through fifth grade general music and the sixth grade choral program in the East Lansing, Michigan, schools. Previously she worked with kindergarten through sixth grade and high school choral music in the Lainseburg, Michigan, schools. She is currently a graduate student at the University of Michigan.

The Middle School and High School Concert Band, High School Marching Band, High School Jazz Band, Music Theory, and High School Full Orchestra protocols were developed by Ryan Hourigan. He is a PhD student in music education and has been involved in preparing undergraduate students for fieldwork observations and teaching at the University of Michigan. Previous to his graduate study, Hourigan was the Director of Music at Benet Academy in Illinois, where he directed the high school concert bands, jazz bands, and marching band. He also developed the Self-Contained Special Education protocol. He is currently completing a graduate cognate in special education at the University of Michigan.

Early Childhood Music

Program/School _____ Teacher _____

Class_____ Time _____ Date_____

Classroom Environment

Making music with young children occurs in many guises. Thus, this guide relies on description and prediction. First, describe the setting, decorations, furniture, equipment, safety precautions, and comfort facilities (lavatory, changing station, water, etc.) Is this setting child-friendly?

Classroom Management

In rich detail, describe the music makers and their activities.

Describe the tall students and their relationship to the shorter students.

Describe the smaller students. Are they mobile? Are they talking? Are they alert?

On a continuum, describe the degree to which this class is formal or informal.

Informal   Formal
(loose and play-like) (sit still, focus on teacher, like a lecture)
1   2   3   4   5

Comments:

On a continuum, describe the degree to which this class is structured or unstructured.

Unstructured   *Structured*
(adults react to children's interest/behaviors)   (all activities are adult-directed)
   1   2   3   4   5

Comments:

Pedagogy

Assuming that the goal of the program is musical, cognitive, kinesthetic, and social development, briefly describe* the content, activities, presentation style, and the children's participation. You might observe only one child and paint a detailed picture of one child's developmental level, or observe the whole class to form a composite of typical behaviors.

Social development:

Vocal development:

Rhythmic development:

---

* Some suggestions for criteria for your descriptions:
Social: relationships child-child and child-adult, sharing, names, etc.
Vocal: pitched sounds, ascending/descending scoops, imitating sounds or timbres, singing patterns and sections of tunes, creating melodies
Rhythm: imitates short (two- to three-beat) patterns, longer (four- to five-beat) patterns, breathes in time, attempts to display pulse, able to keep consistent pulse
Kinesthetic: explores movement exhibiting flow, weight, space, and time; moves core of body, moves limbs parallel or alternating, crosses midpoint, isolates body parts
Cognitive: knows names, knows body parts, discriminates same/different patterns, makes choices in class, demonstrates prediction in class

Kinesthetic development:

Cognitive development:

Musicianship

Using what you know about classroom, instrumental, and choral music K–6 and the readiness needed to be successful in these classes, choose the outliers in the class—the child who seems the most advanced and the child who seems delayed.

Describe what these outliers will bring to their kindergarten music classes.

As different as these two children are, imagine the variety of children in a heterogeneous kindergarten music class of twenty. How might the teacher assess skills and plan musical development for a diverse class of learners?

Elementary General Music

Program/School _____ *Teacher* _____

*Class*_____ *Time* _____ *Date*_____

For each statement circle whether you A–agree, U–are unsure, or D–disagree. Explain.

Classroom Environment

The space is an inviting and safe learning environment.   A   U   D

Explain:

The furnishings are appropriate for the learners and activities.   A   U   D

Explain:

There are visual stimuli that reinforce content.   A   U   D

Explain:

There are learning stations for individual or group work.   A   U   D

Explain:

Teaching materials are organized and accessible.   A   U   D

Explain:

I could see myself teaching in a room like this.   A   U   D

Explain:

Classroom Management/Pedagogy

Learners:

Are motivated to begin the lesson.   A   U   D
Explain:

Exhibit behaviors I anticipated for their age and development. A   U   D
Explain:

Understand what is being asked of them.   A   U   D
Explain:

Seem to have the readiness to be successful in today's tasks. A   U   D
Explain:

Are actively engaged throughout the period.   A   U   D
Explain:

Describe the learner-learner and learner-teacher relationships in comparison to your expectations for behavior and your identity as the teacher.

Describe the skill or knowledge acquisition you've witnessed. How are the learners different as a result of today's instruction?

Lesson Strategy

Goals and structure are evident.   A   U   D

Explain:

The expectations for behavior are clear and consistent.   A   U   D

Explain:

There are consistent consequences for inappropriate behavior.   A   U   D

Explain:

The ratio of positive to negative feedback is beneficial.   A   U   D

Explain:

The ratio of verbiage to music is conducive to learning.   A   U   D

Explain:

The educator is an effective and accurate model.   A   U   D

Explain:

Mastery is achieved before moving to the next activity.   A   U   D

Explain:

Transitions are effective.   A   U   D

Explain:

Closure is achieved and the lesson's successes are celebrated.   A   U   D

Explain:

Describe the manner in which the educator meets the needs of the class as a whole.

Describe the manner in which the educator attends to individual differences:

If you were to summarize this teacher's philosophy in one sentence, it would be: Are you able to identify methods, techniques, or cognitive theories to which this educator subscribes?

Describe a portion of this lesson that you would and could teach.

Describe a portion of this lesson that you would but cannot yet teach.

Additional Observations and Questions to Ask the Teacher

Please flex your intellectual curiosity by asking many diverse questions. Most of what happens in a learning situation doesn't happen by accident, but if it does, that's also interesting to know. Jot down anything you're wondering about. If there is time to ask the person you're observing, this will help you understand all the planning and thought behind classroom activities. If not, you should bring these questions back to the college setting, where they may help put course content into a more meaningful context. Any questions are appropriate, but all the "W" questions are a great way to start:

Why is the room arranged this way? Where did you find that song?
Who were your models? When do you know it's time to move on in the lesson?
What would be the logical follow-up to this lesson?

Beginning Band

Program/School _____ *Teacher* _____

*Class*_____ *Time* _____ *Date*_____

Classroom Environment/Management

While no one expects to see every aspect of a comprehensive program in a single visit, many good programs feature particular elements. Describe those that are evident, and infer those that are not.

Is the room ready when students enter?

Describe the procedures for the students' entering and leaving the room.

Notice students who play an instrument you play, and evaluate the way they handle the cases and assemble the instruments and subsequent packing up. Also notice percussion equipment, set-up, and care.

Note the teacher's tasks prior to the formal beginning of the rehearsal.

How are the folders and music organized?

Are there any instrument equipment disasters?

Estimate what percentage of the rehearsal time is devoted to the category above.

What percentage of the teacher's effort and attention during class is similarly devoted?

Pedagogy/Rehearsal Strategy/Musicianship

While surely there is much to be learned through performance repertoire, many instrumental teachers teach technique, musicianship, notation, comprehension, improvisation, theory, etc., during a portion of the rehearsal. In a few areas, this may be done during small-group lessons or sectionals, independent of rehearsal. Restrict your comments to instruction and activities NOT directly related to a piece of band music for performance.

What is modeled in terms of physical and mental preparation for making music?

Either as a whole or as a section, evaluate tone quality.

1	2	3	4	5
(beginner)	(developing beginner)	(intermediate)	(adv. high school)	(collegiate)

How might tone be improved?

What is the average range of each section?

How do we expand range?

Describe any activities that exercise rhythmic patterns and pulse.

Is movement used to teach rhythm?   Chanting?   Syllables?

Describe any activities that exercise tonal patterns and harmonic sense.

Is singing used to teach pitch?   Are syllables?

Either as a whole or as a section, evaluate intonation.

1	2	3	4	5
(beginner)	(developing beginner)	(intermediate)	(adv. high school)	(collegiate)

Are you able to isolate individuals who do not play in tune or individuals who are out of tune with their sections? Are families of instruments in tune across the ensemble?

Is intonation mentioned? Is there an electronic device being used?

Describe the:

Modeling

Ratio of talking/instructing/correcting (teacher talk) to music making

Overall pace of instruction

Ratio of on- versus off-task behavior

Ratio of rote learning to note reading

Meters present in the musical content

Tonalities and keys present in the musical content

Activities that promote expressive elements in music

Activities that promote improvisation

Is anything else going on?

Piece Rehearsed in Class

Title(s):_____

Composer(s):_____

Brief description of meter, tonality, key, and style:

Where are we in the continuum of learning the piece?

unfamiliar/struggling		familiar/learning		mastery/refining
1	2	3	4	5

What techniques are used to acquaint students with the whole piece, the big picture?

What techniques are used to help students deconstruct the piece into separate elements?

What is the evidence of applying prior knowledge? Presenting new concepts or skills?

Perhaps you have a score or can peer over someone's shoulder. Identify a section in the music that is unperformable and isolated by the teacher. Describe the techniques used to make improvements.

Identify a section in the music that is unperformable, missed, or ignored by the teacher and the techniques you would use to make improvements.

Additional Observations and Questions to Ask the Teacher

Without attacking a personal approach to conducting, comment on the pattern, expressions, and gestures used from the podium.

Was there a lesson/rehearsal plan?

Do most students exhibit the musical readiness to be successful in this repertoire?

To what degree do students contribute, think, and respond in the rehearsal?

Was cooperative learning used during the rehearsal?

Is there a management plan? Are there classroom rules?

Does the teacher ever leave the podium area?

General ratio of positive to negative comments by the teacher: P=   N=

Describe any audio, visual, or technical teaching techniques.

Does this look, sound, and smell like your beginning band experience?

Name one new idea you saw today that you would borrow or vary.

Name one procedure, activity, or comment you would avoid.

Please flex your intellectual curiosity by asking many diverse questions. Most of what happens in a learning situation doesn't happen by accident, but if it does, that's also interesting to know. Jot down anything you're wondering about. If there is time to ask the person you're observing, this will help you understand all the planning and thought behind classroom activities. If not, you should bring these questions back to the college setting, where they may help put course content into a more meaningful context.

Elementary Choral Music

Program/School _____ Teacher _____

Class_____ Time _____ Date_____

Classroom Environment/Management

While no one expects to see every aspect of a comprehensive program in a single visit, many good programs feature particular elements. Describe those that are evident, and infer those that are not.

Is the room ready when students enter?

Describe the procedures for the students' entering and leaving the room.

Note the teacher's tasks prior to the formal beginning of the rehearsal.

If used, how are folders and music organized?

Estimate what percentage of the rehearsal time is devoted to the category above.

What percentage of the teacher's effort goes toward getting the students' attention during class?

Pedagogy/Rehearsal Strategy/Musicianship

While surely there is much to be learned through performance repertoire, many choral teachers teach technique, musicianship, notation, comprehension, improvisation, theory, etc., during a portion of the rehearsal. In a few areas, this may be done during small group lessons, sectionals, or classroom time, independent of the rehearsal. Restrict your comments to instruction and activities NOT directly related to a piece of choral music for performance.

What is modeled in terms of physical and mental preparation for making music?

Is everyone using a singing voice?

Either as a whole or as a section, evaluate tone quality.

1	2	3	4	5
(beginner)	(developing beginner)	(intermediate)	(adv. high school)	(collegiate)

How might tone be improved?

What is the average range of each section?

How do we expand range?

Describe any activities that exercise rhythmic patterns and pulse.

Is movement used to teach rhythm? Chanting? Syllables?

Describe any activities that exercise tonal patterns and harmonic sense.

Are syllables being used?

Either as a whole or a section, evaluate intonation.

1	2	3	4	5
(beginner)	(developing beginner)	(intermediate)	(adv. high school)	(collegiate)

Are you able to isolate individuals who do not sing in tune or individuals out of tune with their sections? Are sections in tune across the ensemble?

Is intonation mentioned?

Describe the:

Modeling

Ratio of talking/instructing/correcting (teacher talk) to music making

Overall pace of instruction

Ratio of on- versus off-task behavior

Ratio of rote learning to note reading

Meters present in the musical content

Tonalities and keys present in the musical content

Activities that promote expressive elements in music

Activities that promote improvisation

Is anything else going on?

Piece Rehearsed in Class

Title(s):_____

Composer(s):_____

Brief description of meter, tonality, key, and style:
Where are we in the continuum of learning the piece?

unfamiliar/struggling		familiar/learning		mastery/refining
1	2	3	4	5

What techniques are used to acquaint students with the whole piece, the big picture?

What techniques are used to help students deconstruct the piece into separate elements?

Is the focus on text, pronunciation, or interpretation?

Is there evidence of applying prior knowledge? Of presenting new concepts or skills?

Perhaps you have a score or can peer over someone's shoulder. Identify a section in the music that is unperformable and isolated by the teacher. Describe the techniques used to make improvements.

Identify a section in the music that is unperformable, missed, or ignored by the teacher and the techniques you would use to make improvement.

Additional Observations and Questions to Ask the Teacher

Without attacking a personal approach to conducting, comment on the pattern, expressions, and gestures used from the podium.

Was there a lesson/rehearsal plan?

Do most students exhibit the musical readiness to be successful on this repertoire?

To what degree do students contribute, think, and respond in the rehearsal?

Was cooperative learning used during the rehearsal?

Is there a management plan? Are there classroom rules?

Does the teacher ever leave the podium area?

Is an accompaniment being used? How much of the time?

Who is providing the accompaniment?

General ratio of positive to negative comments by the teacher: P=   N=

Describe any audio, visual, or technical teaching techniques.

Does this look, sound, and smell like your beginning choral experience?

Name one new idea you saw today that you would borrow or vary.

Name one procedure, activity, or comment you would avoid.

Please flex your intellectual curiosity by asking many diverse questions. Most of what happens in a learning situation doesn't happen by accident, but if it does that's also interesting to know. Jot down anything you're wondering about. If there is time to ask the person you're observing, this will help you understand all the planning and thought behind classroom activities. If not, you should bring these questions back to the college setting, where they may help put course content into a more meaningful context.

Beginning Strings

Program/School _____ *Teacher* _____

*Class*_____ *Time* _____ *Date*_____

Classroom Environment

What is the general classroom set-up?

How do students carry, open, and put away their instruments?

What accessories do they use (e.g., types of shoulder rests, rockstops, rosin, etc.), and how do they teach their use?

Are the students learning something? Are they engaged in the activities?

How does the teacher encourage the students to make musical decisions?

Classroom Management

What is the rapport between the teacher and the students?

How did the teacher start the class? What is the pace? How are the instruments tuned?

Was the teacher able to start the rehearsal in an orderly fashion?

Did you observe any classroom management issues during this class (excessive talking, disorderly behavior, etc.)?

How did the teacher deal with these issues?

How often did the students play music during this lesson?

Pedagogy

How does the teacher address posture, both sitting and standing?

How does the teacher address instrument position, bow-hand position, bow-arm position/movement, left-hand position, and rest position?

What terminology does the teacher use for tone production (e.g., more bow pressure vs. heavier arm weight)?

How often is position reinforced each lesson?

What general strategies does the teacher use to correct mistakes?

How are the students taught intonation? (Fine tuners? Pegs?)

Musicianship

How often do students read music? Learn by rote? When is reading introduced?

When do students start multi-part music? How is it introduced (in sectionals, full class, etc.)?

How often is physical movement taught? Is movement encouraged? How?

How often do students sing?

How is intonation addressed? What terminology is used (i.e., fingers on tape, flat and sharp, higher and lower)?

Additional Observations and Questions to Ask the Teacher

Do they start by playing pizzicato, arco, or a combination of both?

When and how do they introduce left-hand fourth finger for violins and violas?

When and how do they introduce shifting for the basses? For all instruments?

When and how do they introduce extensions for the cellos?

Do bass players learn sitting, standing, or using a combination of the two? In what order are these methods taught?

How and when are students taught the parts of their instruments?

Are beginning players taught long tones or faster rhythms first?

How are key signatures taught in relation to hand shape and position?

What bowing styles are students able to correctly demonstrate?

What method book is used? What other materials are used?

How much practice does the teacher require?

Middle School and High School Strings

Program/School _____ *Teacher* _____

*Class*_____ *Time* _____ *Date*_____

Classroom Environment

What is the general classroom set-up?

Are the students learning something? Are they engaged in the activities?

How does the teacher encourage the students to make musical decisions?

Classroom Management

What is the rapport between the teacher and the students?

What is the start-up routine (tuning, physical warm-up, scales, method book)?

Did you observe any classroom management issues (excessive talking, disorderly behavior, etc.)? How did the teacher deal with these issues?

Pedagogy

What is the ratio of piece rehearsing to technique training?

What bowing styles are students able to correctly demonstrate?

How does the director address shifting, right-hand position, and left-hand position in relation to key signatures?

Rehearsal Strategy

Does the director share his or her rehearsal strategies with the students?

Does the director share his or her strategies verbally or in a written form (on the board, etc.)?

Are the rehearsal objectives attainable by this group?

Are the directions given from the podium clear and concise?

Does the director value student input on rehearsal strategy?

Musicianship

When and how are students taught to tune?

How often do they talk about technique vs. musicality?

How often do students lead rehearsals (e.g., sectionals)?

Additional Observations and Questions to Ask the Teacher

When and how is vibrato taught?

What method book is used?

How much and what kind of practice is required?

When/how are students taught to shift? What positions are used?

How are students taught to play with conducting?

What literature is performed?

How often do they perform?

High School Full Orchestra

Program/School _____ *Teacher* _____

Class _____ *Time* _____ *Date* _____

Classroom Environment

Is the rehearsal room clean and organized?

Were the chairs and music stands set up prior to the rehearsal?

Do students have easy access to instruments and music?

Did set-up or access problems affect the start of rehearsal?

Classroom Management

What was the rapport between the teacher and the students?

How did the teacher start the rehearsal?

Was the teacher able to start the rehearsal in an orderly fashion?

Did you observe any classroom management issues (excessive talking, disorderly behavior, etc.)?

How did the teacher deal with these issues?

How often did the students play music during this lesson?

Rehearsal Strategy

Does the director share his or her rehearsal strategies with the students?

Does the director share his or her strategies verbally or in a written form (on the board, etc.)?

Are the rehearsal objectives attainable by this group?

Are the directions given from the podium clear and concise?

Does the director value student input on rehearsal strategies?

Pedagogy

Did the director warm up the group? How?

How does the director approach breathing with the winds?

What is the terminology used to discuss pedagogy in winds versus strings?

What is the tuning sequence? To what pitch do they tune? Using what instrument? Who leads the tuning procedure?

How does the director address ensemble pitch?

Does the director have the students play in various key centers?

How does the director address issues of balance?

Does the director address executive skills (posture, hand position, embouchure, etc.)?

Musicianship

Does the director have a clear understanding of the score?

Does the director communicate these ideas to the ensemble?

Are his or her patterns clear?

Is the director helping the ensemble with his or her conducting?

How often do they talk about technique vs. musicality?

Additional Observations and Questions for the Teacher

How is full orchestra scheduled? How often and when do they rehearse?

What method is used to work on basic group fundamentals (balance, articulation, etc.)?

How often does the group perform?

Which wind and percussion students are in full orchestra?

Middle School and High School General Music

Program/School _____ *Teacher* _____

*Class*_____ *Time* _____ *Date*_____

Classroom Environment

How are the students physically organized and seated in the class (desks, chairs, stations)?

Is the room inviting, and is subject-related material posted in the room?

Classroom Management/Pedagogy

What are the procedures for entering and exiting the classroom?

Are there classroom rules posted clearly in the room? Are they enforced? If there are no rules posted, can implied, consistent rules be observed?

How are materials, manipulatives, or instruments acquired or passed out to students?

What materials or resources are used?

How are directions given to students (verbal or non-verbal)?

What are the procedures for evaluating student responses (individual/group) (written/anecdotal)?

If there are procedures for evaluating students' responses, what skills are being evaluated?

What is the balance between active music making and learning "about" music?

Are there procedures the teacher has established to focus student attention? To focus individuals? The group?

Are there certain consistent cues given to students to indicate success or lack thereof on the part of the students?

What components of the classroom's physical organization contribute to management?

Teaching Strategies

How does the arrangement of various activities contribute to the pacing of the lesson plan?

How many activities are teacher-directed vs. student-directed?

Are there opportunities for individual musical responses by students?

How does the lesson appear to be organized? By the number of activities? By the type or variety (e.g., movement, singing, instruments, listening, theory, reading/writing, creativity, composition/improvisation)?

Are the students focused and actively engaged in the activities?

Does the teacher employ an obvious methodology or methodologies?

Name specific genres of music experienced during class (rock, rap, classical, bluegrass, jazz, opera, etc.)

Additional Observations and Questions to Ask the Teacher

Is there a music curriculum in the district?

Is the curriculum aligned with the MENC National Standards?

Is the curriculum user-friendly?

Is the curriculum consistently used as a reference for the teacher?

Is the curriculum connected to the evaluations employed by the teacher?

Is the curriculum connected to the report cards used by the teacher?

Are the teacher's evaluations connected to the report cards?

Are concerts mandatory in the school district? What form do they take, and what is their frequency?

How often does the teacher have programs or concerts, if at all?

If the teacher has programs or concerts, at what grade levels? What formats do the programs take?

Does the teacher have any additional certificates, and what where the motivations behind seeking additional certification?

Who are the students in this class? Is the course required?

Middle School and High School Choral Music

Program/School _____ *Teacher* _____

*Class*_____ *Time* _____ *Date*_____

Classroom Environment

How are materials organized and passed out (student folders, etc.)?

How are the students arranged within the classroom (chairs, risers; sitting, standing; by voice part)?

Is an accompanist used during rehearsals? For concerts?

Classroom Management

How does the teacher interact with the students (use of humor, engaging individuals, motivation through personal connection)?

Is the teacher able to communicate and apply consistent behavioral or procedural expectations? Describe ways the teacher accomplishes this communication during rehearsals.

63

Is the teacher able to use encouraging, positive, constructive feedback, while clearly defining the need for change or improvement? Give an example of how this is achieved.

Describe the pace of the rehearsal and how this affects the behavior of the students. Is there an obvious plan of action communicated to the students, and how is this communicated? Are there smooth transitions between activities and songs?

Pedagogy/Rehearsal Strategy

How much time is allotted for warm-ups?

What is the focus of warm-ups? Resonance? Range expansion? Agility? Diction? Vowel unification?

Are warm-ups related to the literature used in rehearsals?

How much time is allotted to sight-reading? How frequently do the students sight-read?

What system do the students use for reading (tonal/rhythm syllables, unison or number parts)?

What strategies are used to teach parts to the students during warm-ups, sight-reading, and rehearsal? Solfege? Sectionals? Rote learning? Use of piano or voice? Verbal or spoken directions? Vocal demonstration? Movement? Visual aids?

Is there a specific focus (e.g., pitch, intonation; tone, resonance; diction, articulation, and enunciation; phrasing and expression; breath support; or posture) on choral technique, and how does the director accomplish this?

Is there a mix of focus on the whole and the parts of each song?

Is there variety in the repertoire? Are there multicultural, sacred, secular, folk tune, and lighter numbers? Are there polyphonic (partner songs, rounds, etc.) and homophonic songs?

How does the teacher address the needs of the changing voice?

Is the rehearsal mainly teacher-driven/directed or student-driven/directed?

When giving directions during rehearsals, how many issues are addressed at one time?

Musicianship

Does the director have a clear conducting pattern, effective cues, artistic interpretation, and purposeful gestures?

Describe the director's piano skills.

Describe the director's vocal skills.

Do the students clearly understand and communicate the text of the literature?

Additional Observations and Questions to Ask the Teacher

How does the teacher communicate with the parents?

Does the teacher make use of a handbook?

Does the ensemble participate in festivals or competitions?

Are concerts mandatory in the school district? What form do they take, and what is their frequency?

What types of vocal ensembles are available to the students (e.g., audition/ non-audition, male/female/mixed, a capella, madrigal/chamber/select)?

How are students assessed? What skills are assessed and how? Are students assessed as individuals or in a group?

How are grades determined?

What are the criteria for choosing literature?

Middle School and High School Band

Program/School _____ *Teacher* _____

*Class*_____ *Time* _____ *Date*_____

Classroom Environment

Is the band room clean and organized?

Were the chairs and music stands set up prior to the rehearsal?

Do students have easy access to instruments and music?

Did set-up or access problems affect the start of the rehearsal?

Classroom Management

How did the teacher start the rehearsal?

Was the teacher able to start the rehearsal in an orderly fashion?

Did you observe any classroom management issues (excessive talking, disorderly behavior, etc.)?

How did the teacher deal with these issues?

How often did the students play music during this lesson?

Pedagogy

Did the director warm up the group? How?

How does the director approach breathing?

Does the director use a method book (chorales, technique builder, etc.)?

Is there a tuning sequence at warm-up?

How does the director address ensemble pitch?

Does the director have the students play in various key centers?

Does the director talk about a sound concept (pyramid of sound, etc.)?

Does the director address executive skills (posture, hand position, positive embouchure, etc.)?

Rehearsal Strategy

Does the director share his or her rehearsal strategies with the students?

Does the director share his or her strategies verbally or in written form (on the board, etc.)?

Are the rehearsal objectives attainable by this group?

Are the directions given from the podium clear and concise?

Does the director value student input on rehearsal strategy?

Musicianship

Does the director have a clear understanding of the score?

Does the director communicate these ideas to the ensemble? Are his or her patterns clear?

Is the director helping the ensemble with his or her conducting?

Additional Observations and Questions to Ask the Teacher

Is the director able to connect with the students?

Do the students respect the director?

Do you feel that the students think they have accomplished something during this rehearsal?

Would you have liked to be in this band?

Middle School and High School Jazz Band

Program/School _____ *Teacher* _____

*Class*_____ *Time* _____ *Date*_____

Classroom Environment

Is the rehearsal space clean and organized?

Were the chairs, music stands, and rhythm section equipment set up prior to the rehearsal?

Do students have easy access to instruments and music?

Did set up or access problems affect the start of rehearsal?

How is the ensemble set up?

How is the rhythm section (piano, bass, guitar, and drums) set up?

Classroom Management

How did the teacher start the rehearsal?

Was the teacher able to start the rehearsal in an orderly fashion?

Were there any classroom management issues you observed (excessive talking, disorderly behavior, etc.)?

How did the teacher deal with these issues?

How often did the students play music during this rehearsal?

Pedagogy

Did the director warm up the group? How?

Does the director use a method book (improvisation method, etc.)?

Is there a tuning sequence at warm-up?

How does the director address ensemble pitch?

Does the director have the students play in various key centers?

Does the director talk about a sound concept?

How does the director address incorporating the rhythm section into the ensemble sound and pulse?

How does the director teach improvisation?

Rehearsal Strategy

Does the director share his or her rehearsal strategies with the students?

Does the director share his or her strategies verbally or in a written form (on the board, etc.)?

Are the rehearsal objectives attainable by this group?

Are the directions given by the director clear and concise?

Does the director value student input on rehearsal strategies?

Does the director incorporate listening to recordings in rehearsals?

Musicianship

Does the director have a clear understanding of the score?

Does the director communicate these ideas to the ensemble? How?

Does the director have a clear understanding of different styles (Latin, swing, etc.)? Is the director able to communicate these concepts to the rhythm section?

Does the director model stylistic considerations on his or her instrument?

Additional Observations and Questions for the Director

Is the director able to connect with the students?

Do the students respect the director?

Do you feel that the students feel as though they have accomplished something during this rehearsal?

Would you have liked to be in this band?

Is the group extracurricular?

What kind of events does this group play for (concerts, festivals, gigs, etc.)?

How are students chosen to be a part of this group?

How are soloists chosen?

How do you recruit rhythm section players?

High School Marching Band (Outdoor Rehearsal)

Program/School _____ *Teacher* _____

*Class*_____ *Time* _____ *Date*_____

Classroom Management

How did the teacher start the rehearsal?

Was the teacher able to start the rehearsal in an orderly fashion?

Were there any classroom management issues you observed (excessive talking, disorderly behavior, etc.)?

How did the teacher deal with these issues?

How often did the students play music during this lesson?

Pedagogy

Did the director warm up the group? How?

Are marching fundamentals a part of this warm-up?

How does the director approach breathing?

Is there a tuning sequence at warm-up?

How does the director address ensemble pitch?

Does the director talk about a sound concept (pyramid of sound, etc.)?

Does the director address executive skills (posture, hand position, positive embouchure, etc.)?

Rehearsal Strategy

Does the director share his or her rehearsal strategies with the students?

Does the director share his or her strategies verbally or in a written form (on the board, on the way out to the field, etc.)?

Are the rehearsal objectives attainable by this group?

Are the directions given from the podium clear and concise?

Does the director value student input on rehearsal strategy?

Is this band competitive in nature?

How does the director address marching fundamentals? Are they Big 10- or corps-style fundamentals?

How does the director approach moving and playing?

How does the band learn drill? Is there a method?

Musicianship

Does the director have a clear understanding of the show?

Does the director communicate these ideas to the ensemble?

Does the director have a clear understanding of the drill?

Is the director able to clearly communicate his or her ideas to the ensemble?

How is ensemble pulse (fazing) addressed?

How does the director incorporate student leadership into rehearsals (section leaders, drum majors, etc.)?

What responsibilities were given to these student leaders (attendance, organizational work, cleaning drill, etc.)?

Did the other students seem to respect these leaders?

Did you notice any anecdotal evidence of this?

Additional Observations and Questions to Ask the Teacher

Is the director able to connect with the students?

Do the students respect the director?

Does it seem that the students feel as though they have accomplished something?

Would you have liked to be in this band?

How do students earn leadership positions in the marching band?

Do they go through any training?

How does the director choose music?

Who writes the drill?

Does the teacher use any technology (drill-design programs, etc.)?

What are summer rehearsals like (band camp, etc.)?

High School Music Theory

Program/School _____ *Teacher* _____

*Class*_____ *Time* _____ *Date*_____

Classroom Environment/Management

What are the curricular goals of the class?

Is this a music theory class or a combined music theory and aural training class?

Are all students allowed to enroll in this class? If not, how are they given permission to enroll? Are they given full credit toward graduation?

Is composition part of this class?

What textbooks are used in this class?

Is there a workbook or a supplement?

Does the instructor use any computer software?

Does this classroom have the capability to accommodate the technological needs of the class? Do they go to a computer lab? How often?

Pedagogy

Does the instructor have a clear understanding of the topic?

How was the lesson structured (lecture, group work, individual work time, etc.)?

How does the instructor teach to the different ability levels?

Do the students seem to like the class? Why?

How are the students assessed in this class?

Is it formative or summative or both?

Do the students in this class take the AP exam for music theory at the end of the school year?

How are the students graded?

Is it difficult to prepare for this class?

How does the teacher offer individual help?

How did the teacher learn the technology involved with this class?

Additional Observations and Questions to Ask the Teacher

Are most of these students aspiring music majors?

Do you get a chance to teach students whom you would normally not see?

Was this a class that you started at this school? If so, how did you sell the idea to the administration?

Self-Contained Special Education

Program/School _____ Teacher _____

Class_____ Time _____ Date_____

Classroom Environment/Management

What are the goals of this special education room? (Find out prior to the observation.)

What kinds of disabilities do these students have (cognitive, behavioral, physical)?

What is the ratio of teachers and aides to students in this classroom?

How often is music incorporated into the curriculum?

How often do these students have music with a specialist?

Teaching Strategy/Musicianship

Do the students like the music lesson?

Do the students respond to the music teacher?

How does the teacher engage the students with music?

What musical skills are they learning?

Do the teachers and the aides assist the students during the lesson?

Additional Observations and Questions to Ask the Music Teacher and the Special Education Teacher

Music Teacher:

Have you had any preparation in learning to teach students with special needs?

What is your relationship with the classroom teacher like? Do you discuss strategies?

Do you adapt your lessons for this class? How?

Have you been involved in the IEP process for your students?

Special Education Teacher:

How does music fit into your curricular goals for this class?

How do you use music when the music specialist is not here (sing to the students, play recorded music, etc.)?

Non-Traditional Ensembles

Program/School _____ *Teacher* _____

*Class*_____ *Time* _____ *Date*_____

Classroom Environment/Management

As time permits, learn about the following organizational and procedural aspects. How did this ensemble come to exist?

Who may join? How?

What is the rehearsal schedule?

Is performance the goal? If so, how are performances organized? If not, is there some sort of culminating experience?

Pedagogy

Everything was non-traditional at some point; your class may not even agree to the definition of non-traditional! Thus, this category is a catch-all to include "all other options" or perhaps "things we weren't taught how to do." As such, this form is necessarily open-ended. Please supplement with rich description regarding your specific experience. Additional ensembles are music educators' means for meeting the needs of students or a community—a new vehicle through which to convey musical understanding.

Describe the music that is being made (or general performance characteristics): instruments, voices, size of group, movement, or dramatic components, etc.

In what ways, e.g., form, meter, tonality, style, is this music similar to music used in typical bands, choruses, and orchestras? To current commercial or folk music?

In what ways is it different?

Does this music draw from a particular culture, ethnicity, or lifestyle?

Are there extramusical elements of the culture being taught? Are there attempts at authenticity?

Are there unique musical aspects that can be learned only, or more efficiently, through this ensemble?

Describe the age, ethnicity, and style of students in the ensemble. How do they compare with students in other musical ensembles? With the general student population?

Teaching Strategy

Describe the leadership. Is a teacher present? Is there a student leader or leadership through consensus? Is this a smooth process? What does it remind you of?

How are organizational and musical decisions reached?

Is music being taught? If so, is transmission mostly by rote or by note? What is most authentic to the style of the music?

Have you had an opportunity to participate in groups such as this? Would you like to?

Can you see any themes from classes such as world music, sociology, popular culture, world history, or your personal life being enacted in this ensemble?

Additional Observations and Questions to Ask the Teacher

How do the members feel about their experience with the group?

From where does the group draw music, inspiration, and models?

Is there funding for this activity?

Do you have unique interests or talents to share in such an ensemble? How might you organize it so that it is a valuable part of students' musical experience and advances your overall philosophy of music education?

Research Base for Fieldwork as an Undergraduate Student

Barry, N. 1996. Promoting reflective practice in an elementary music methods course. *Journal of Music Teacher Education* 5(2): 6–13.

Butler, A. 2001. Preservice teachers' conceptions of teaching effectiveness, microteaching experiences, and teaching performance. *Journal of Research in Music Education* 49(3): 258–272.

Campbell, M. R. 1999. Learning to teach: A collaborative ethnography. *Bulletin of the Council for Research in Music Education* 139: 12–36.

Conkling, S. W. 2003. Uncovering preservice music teachers' reflective thinking: Making sense of learning to teach. *Bulletin of the Council for Research in Music Education* 155: 11–23.

Conkling, S. W., and W. Henry. 1999. Professional development partnerships: A new model for music teacher preparation. *Arts Education Policy Review* 100(4): 19–23.

Henry, W. 2001. Music teacher education and the professional development school. *Journal of Music Teacher Education* 10(2): 23–28.

Kerchner, J. L. 1998. A model for educational partnerships. *Journal of Music Teacher Education* 8(1): 7–14.

Reynolds, A., and C. M. Conway. 2003. Service-learning in music education methods: Perceptions of participants. *Bulletin of the Council for Research in Music Education* 155: 1–10.

Thompson, L. K. 2000. Freshmen music education majors' preconceived beliefs about the people and processes involved in teaching. PhD diss., University of Arizona.

Townsend, R. D. 2000. The holmes group: A private college plausibility study. *Journal of Music Teacher Education* 10(1): 24–31.

Suggested Readings for Fieldwork as an Undergraduate Student

Erwin, J., K. Edwards, J. Kerchner, and J. Knight. 2003. *Prelude to music education.* Upper Saddle River, NJ: Pearson.

Roe, B. D., and E. P. Ross. 2002. *Student teaching and field experiences handbook.* 5th ed. Upper Saddle River, NJ: Prentice-Hall.

Wragg, E. C. 1999. *An introduction to classroom observation.* 2nd ed. New York: Routledge.

Part Two:

Student Teaching in Music

Chapter Four
Preparing for Student Teaching

The Placement Process

The process of placement for student teaching varies by institution. However, there are some general concepts that are similar across schools. Most require an application procedure for student teaching. There is usually a deadline for application, and there are a certain number of courses that must be completed before student teaching. Some music departments require proficiency exams on secondary instruments or piano. In some settings, standardized state teacher examinations must be completed and passed before student teaching. Sometimes CPR is required. Chapter Seven includes information regarding which exams and requirements are necessary for certification in each state and suggestions for preparing for these exams.

In several institutions student teacher placement is handled by the education department, and the music student teachers have little choice in selecting the placement. In other programs student teachers choose the length of a placement and the type of music classroom in which they will spend time. In certain cases, students even make the final choice regarding with whom they will student teach.

At the state and/or school district level, some settings require student teachers/teacher candidates to be fingerprinted. Many states require special courses on child abuse, state history, or other topics. Some institutions require these criteria before certification, while others require them before student teaching. The line between issues of certification and issues of clearance for student teaching is sometimes gray.

In some states the number of hours and ages of children worked with in student teaching are carefully dictated by the state. The department or school of education will usually have one staff member who is the contact for all questions regarding state certification and student teaching. The application for student teaching may be within the college or department of education, or it may be within the music education division. Find out what the policies are for your program. Don't wait for this information to come to you. Be proactive early on in your degree program so you are sure to be ready for the student teaching placement process when the time comes.

Advantages and Disadvantages of Various Models of Student Teaching

As important as student teaching is, it is never perfect. The student teacher must recognize that there will be many inauthentic aspects of student teaching. The students and the classroom are not really "yours" during student teaching, and some student teachers find that quite uncomfortable. There are advantages and disadvantages to every decision made regarding student teaching placement. No one placement can offer all that the student teacher hopes to experience.

Most states require that student teachers in music work with children of different age groups throughout the semester. One of the decisions that must be made is how the placement will be arranged so as to ensure that the student gets this experience. Again, there is no one perfect model. A student teacher might work with elementary children in one school district for a certain number of weeks and then go to a completely different school district as a secondary placement. Or the student teacher might stay in one district for the entire placement and divide days between elementary and secondary students. Student teachers could work three days a week in one setting and two days a week in another. They might work for half the placement in one setting and for half the placement in another. The possibilities are endless.

Some feel that working in different school districts offers more variety for student teachers because they get to see how classrooms work in two settings. We have had students choose to go to two very different types of schools (e.g., eight weeks in large urban school and eight weeks in a suburban school) to really take advantage of the diversity. However, this model has the disadvantage that the teacher is with students for a shorter period of time and has less opportunity to really get to know them.

A placement that is in the same setting for the entire time allows student teachers more of a chance to get to know students and to grow as a teacher. However, there is less opportunity to examine various models and strategies. In many states certification for music covers P–12, and some student teachers try to find a placement that will allow maximum opportunity in all areas of music education (band, strings, choral, etc.). The advantage to this is that the student teacher gets at least some familiarity with all aspects of music education. However, the time spent in each may be so insignificant that the student teacher does not really feel comfortable with any subject matter.

In the traditional one-semester, trimester, or quarter student teaching model the student must make some decisions regarding whether to student teach during the first term or during the second. These choices are often dictated by other coursework and schedules. However, it is important to recognize the different experiences gained during different times of the year. For instrumental music, the fall is an important time to work with beginning instrumentalists in their first few lessons. By January, they are really no longer beginners. Many high school band programs have a heavy focus on marching band in the fall and on contests and festivals in the spring. These are very different kinds of experiences. Choral students who intern during work on a musical have a different experience from those teaching at another time. In elementary general music, fall student teachers get to experience the set-up of the classroom with regard to classroom management in a way that spring student teachers do not. This is true for the fall set-up in all music classrooms. Student teachers should recognize what is missing from each experience just based on the time of year.

If possible, make arrangements to observe the potential placement site so you can get a sense of the program, the students, and the co-operating teacher. Try to visualize yourself in that school. Ask yourself if this is an environment where you will be able to learn. As has been mentioned before, there are no perfect placements. Sometimes working in a setting that is completely different from where you have been before offers a great opportunity for learning. In other situations, a setting that is too unfamiliar will be too challenging for the student teacher.

School District Interview for Student Teaching

Many school districts require an interview for student teaching. You will most likely schedule the interview with the co-operating teacher, and you may interview with a principal or district office administrator at the same time. This interview is a way for the co-operating teacher and the building or district administrator to get to know you and to consider whether they feel they could work with you. It is also an opportunity for you to get a further sense of the school, the music program, and the ideals of the co-operating teacher. Remember, no placement is perfect. There will no doubt be aspects of the school or the program that you find undesirable, but you must decide if the site is a place where you can learn, regardless of some of these issues.

Expect the interview to focus primarily on what you have learned in your preservice coursework and the experiences you have gained in the fieldwork you may have done in conjunction with those courses. It is important to talk about specific musical examples and specific students in this interview if you can. Some sample questions might include:

- What are your goals for the student teaching experience?
- What have you learned about yourself as a teacher in your preservice fieldwork?
- What do you expect to be your greatest challenges in student teaching?
- What are your plans after graduation?

Chapter Eight provides sample interview questions for your first job. Many of these interview questions may be similar to those in the student teaching interview.

Be professional in this interaction. First impressions are important. Dress professionally, and be on time. Bring a copy of your resume to the interview.

Meeting the Students in Advance of the First Day

In some settings, you may be asked to teach or conduct as part of the interview process. Choral students are often asked to demonstrate piano skills. You may want to ask about this in advance so that you can prepare. In other settings you may be hired to work at band camp or to assist with some music program months in advance of the official start of the student teaching. Be sure to keep all these interactions professional. Introduce yourself to students as Mr. or Ms., and begin to model the teacher role regardless of the type of interaction. In the past, we have had students who taught privately in a school district for several years, so students there are familiar with them and on a first-name basis. In these cases it is important to ask these private students to address you as a teacher (Mr. or Ms.) when they are in a school setting.

Final Preparation

As you make decisions regarding student teaching, continue to focus on your emerging personal style as a teacher. Through your preservice fieldwork, you have no doubt begun to get a sense of your strengths and weaknesses. Remember that no student teaching placement will be perfect, and there are things to learn in all types of settings and with all types of co-operating teachers. Be prepared to make the most of whatever your situation offers.

In the last few weeks before the placement begins be sure to check your wardrobe to see that you have proper clothing for full-time teaching. You will need a reliable car and an alarm clock. Get your personal business in order. Be sure you are still covered by university health insurance. Work on piano skills and/or secondary instruments. Double-check the phone and e-mail of your co-operating teacher and other student teachers from your institution.

The final section of this chapter discusses the development of the student teaching portfolio. We suggest that the preservice teacher begin portfolio development during the methods class sequence as many of the projects that are typically required for methods classes are good items for the portfolio. However, it is certainly possible to begin portfolio development during student teaching or even after student teaching is completed. We have opted to include it in this chapter because we believe that the earlier the student begins gathering materials for the teaching portfolio, the easier it will be to put together. Chapter Eight includes more information about many of the issues mentioned in portfolio discussion (e.g., development of a resume and interviewing for a job as a music teacher).

Development of the Student Teaching Portfolio

In some teacher education programs there are very specific requirements for the submission of a student teaching portfolio. These types of portfolios are often process oriented and are designed to show the growth of the student teacher. Other programs encourage the creation of a teaching portfolio for you to bring to a job interview. This is a more product-oriented collection of materials. This chapter focuses on the product type of portfolio. The portfolio presented here will be used in job interviews (addressed in Chapter Eight).

Some school districts require the submission of a teaching portfolio. Others will be happy to look at it if you bring it. Some districts will say nothing in their job description about a portfolio and then ask you for one in the interview. Because many school districts have moved to an all online application process, it may be useful for you to create an e-portfolio on a personal Web site (see "E-Portfolios for the Internet Job Hunt" by Fred Kersten in the February 2004 *Teaching Music*). It is best to be prepared with a reasonable teaching portfolio in the event that you are asked to present one. Whether you create a hard copy or electronic portfolio, it must look professional and organized and be easy to read. All materials in the portfolio should be typed, as should all organizers or headings. For the hard copy version, purchase an attractive black or leather notebook binder that allows you to add and remove materials easily. The following sections may be included (every teacher will have a slightly different portfolio based on his or her individual strengths and experiences).

Portfolio Organization

Resume or Curriculum Vitae
See Chapter Eight for more information regarding resume development.

Copy of State Certification

Copy of Results from State Teacher Exams

Copy of College Transcripts

Copies of Letters of Recommendation

We suggest that you have no more than four letters of recommendation in the portfolio.

Statement of Music Teaching Philosophy

Keep this short—one ore two paragraphs. Present the value of a comprehensive music education, and focus on student-centered learning. Avoid statements such as "I think" or "I believe." Use a philosophical statement that reflects broad concepts of music education and community connections. Avoid language that covers only one aspect of music education (e.g., band, orchestra, choir) in favor of music for all children.

Sample Lesson Plans

For elementary music, we suggest a sample plan for each grade level you have worked with. For ensembles, sample rehearsal plans and/or score study documents are appropriate. Clear connections to state frameworks and national standards should be apparent. Although we do not recommend a specific lesson plan or rehearsal plan format, these materials should include a list of instructional materials, musical goals for the lesson, some sort of time schedule for the class, strategies for instruction, and ideas regarding assessment of student learning.

Sample Development of Curricular Units

Future employers are interested in examples from your planning that represent long-term units or goals. Try to show your understanding of scope and sequence for a particular area of music instruction. You might show a unit of eight or nine weeks for a particular music class or an outline of goals for a specific music class for the school year. If you did not develop these materials in a methods class, work to collect and/or develop them during the student teaching experience.

Sample Assessment Tools

Include any ratings scales, rubrics, or tests you have developed for use in music classes. It is best if the assessment tools relate to something in either your sample lesson plans or your sample curricular unit. Collect these materials from your co-operating teacher throughout the student teaching semester, and include assessment tools you have used even if your co-operating teacher developed them.

Sample Grading Procedures

Put down on paper some of your ideas regarding student grading in ensembles and music classes. This is a common area of discussion in job interviews, and if you have a sample grading outline in your portfolio it can be useful to speak from. If you have developed a large-ensemble handbook or lists of rules and grading procedures, include these as well.

Sample Concert Program with Program Notes

If you had the opportunity to put together a concert program while student teaching, include at least one of the programs in your portfolio. Be creative, and make this sample program something an administrator would be proud to have the school's name on. If you did not do a program for student teaching or in a methods class, generate a sample program for the portfolio.

Sample Music Technology Project

There should be something in your portfolio that represents your knowledge of and experience with instructional technology. This might be an arrangement you wrote and notated using Finale or Sibelius or some other notation software or a marching band drill developed with instructional technology. This could also include samples of student work from a unit on music composition using technology. If you have developed an e-portfolio on a personal Web site, list the link in your hard copy portfolio.

Lists of Educational Performance Literature and Repertoire

Sometimes job interviews focus a great deal on the literature you might choose for a performing group. Having lists of literature with you in a portfolio makes this topic easier to address in the interview. If you have not collected lists of literature in methods classes, begin to collect these lists during student teaching. Many literature lists are available on the Web. Your portfolio could include a list of Web sites for instructional literature.

Sample of Personal Reflection on Teaching

The portfolio may include a written personal reflection of a single teaching event or day of student teaching. Future employers want to know that you are aware of what you do well and what you will need to learn. They know that a beginning teacher does not come to the job with ready-made knowledge and skills, and they want to see you discuss your weaknesses and your strategies for improvement.

Photos

If possible, get photos of yourself working with students in a music setting. Some schools have very strict rules regarding student photographs, so be sure you have permission before including student photos in a portfolio.

Student Work and/or Notes from Students and Parents

It may be appropriate to include some samples of the written work from your students or notes you have received from students or parents. If you have copies of student compositions or essays written by your students regarding their work, include these in the portfolio.

Examples of Your Work as a Musician

Copies of your senior recital program or photos of you on the podium student teaching are great examples of personal musicianship to include in a portfolio. Include just a few examples, as you want to make it clear that you are a music teacher—a musician who teaches. You do not want them to think you are more interested in performance than in teaching.

Videotape of Teaching

Many school districts will ask for a videotape of your teaching as part of the initial submission of materials. Some search committees will view the videotapes and choose candidates to interview based on the tapes. Most committees are interested in seeing you teach, not perform. So do not make the entire tape a concert or performance. Include some examples of your work in an instructional setting. The tape need not be longer than twenty to thirty minutes. If you have worked with students at varying age levels, include short examples of your work in a variety of settings.

Chapter Five
The Working Process
of Student Teaching

Every college or university has its own requirements regarding materials submitted during student teaching. Laws and procedures regarding the experience are different from state to state as well. The student teacher must always remember that there are lessons to be learned in any situation—good or bad.

Laws and Procedures

There are many school district, state, and university laws and procedures that a student teacher must be aware of, including emergency procedures, substitute teaching policies, use of student confidential records, union issues, and teacher professional behavior codes. It is important that the student teacher become familiar with all of these laws and procedures.

Emergency procedures. Make yourself aware before the first day of student teaching of the emergency policies of the school and the classroom in which you will be working. Find out about any students with special health problems. Learn the name of the principal, the custodian, and the school secretary.

Substitute policies. It is important that the student teacher know regulations regarding substitutes. In some states, student teachers cannot be legal substitute teachers and are not to ever be left alone in the room with students. Other states and/or districts allow student teachers to be substitute teachers if they have completed substitute applications. Some colleges and universities will not allow a student teacher to be a substitute even if the state allows it. Be sure to find out what the policy is. The co-operating teacher may not know the policy.

Use of student confidential records. Student teachers must find out the district policy regarding confidential school records. In some cases the student teacher may not be privy to certain records without consent of the student, guardian, or parent.

If a student teacher is allowed access to confidential records (grade reports, test scores, student files) the student teacher must be sure to manage that data in a professional, tactful, and confidential way.

Union issues. Student teachers are not yet members of the teacher's union. They should not participate in work stoppages, sanctions, strikes, lockouts, or other events. Be aware of your university's plan of action if such events take place at the school while you are student teaching.

Teacher professional behavior codes. Student teachers are held to the same professional behavior codes as any teacher in the building. Be sure you are aware of district codes regarding social standards, dress, attendance, use of appropriate language, and relationships with students.

Your First Few Days

Once the student teaching "officially" begins we suggest you find a way to demonstrate your musicianship to the students early on in the placement. We recommend that the co-operating teacher ask the student teacher to play or sing for P–12 students as a way of introduction and as a way to build credibility and respect.

The first few days of student teaching will be spent observing the co-operating teacher and getting to know the students. Some co-operating teachers will support a trial-by-fire start where they put you up in front of large classes for entire class periods in the first few days. Most of us in higher education try to avoid co-operating teachers with that mentality, but sometimes you will find yourself in that setting. If this is your co-operating teacher, do the best you can.

Take advantage of the "observation" time. Take careful notes about what you see and hear, and ask lots of questions of the co-operating teacher. The teacher wants to hear what you are noticing and what types of questions you are able to generate. Many student teachers feel that they do not need this observation time because they have completed fieldwork in other settings. The student teacher must remember that the co-operating teacher most likely has very specific ways of doing things. Respect this, and learn the ropes of that classroom.

Be proactive during the early days, and get involved with students right away. Don't wait for the co-operating teacher to ask you to help. For example, as elementary band students come into the room for a rehearsal, wander around the room and help them get reeds in the right place. Fix hand position and posture. Assist in setting up the room, moving pianos and doing whatever needs to be done.

Many student teachers feel like they are asked to do the grunt work of the teaching job (photocopying, filing music, etc.) in the early days. Although we have seen some co-operating teachers who do assign too much of this work, the student teacher must remember that photocopying and filing music are a part of the job. When there is no student teacher, the co-operating teacher does that work. This is also a good time to secure video equipment either through the school or through the university. You will want to begin videotaping your teaching as early as possible.

Running errands around the building is a great way to get to know the other teachers and the school staff. Take on every task with energy, and show the co-operating teacher how interested you are in being successful—on the podium (or in the classroom) and off.

During the first few days we suggest starting a student teaching questions journal. Keep a note pad with you at all times, and write down questions to ask the co-operating teacher later in the day. As discussed in the first part of this book, it is important to observe while thinking about what may have come before or after. Use the protocols provided in Chapter Three to help you look at all the issues of the classroom from the teacher's perspective. Take note of priorities addressed by the co-operating teacher so that you can model your teaching after what the students are accustomed to. Co-operating teachers often get frustrated if you deviate radically from overall classroom priorities.

Make sure that the questions in no way call into question the abilities of the co-operating teacher. Be careful how you word your questions so that you are collegial and respectful. You will no doubt disagree with your co-operating teacher on many issues. Learn to take what you can from the co-operating teacher, and keep your negative thoughts to yourself. If you want to try something new with students, go over these ideas with your co-operating teacher first. It is important to remember that long after you have completed your student teaching, the co-operating teacher will still be at that school with those students and may not want you to try ideas that they cannot follow through.

Extracurricular Responsibilities

Music teaching includes many rehearsals and classes that meet outside of the school day. During student teaching it is important for the student teacher to get a realistic vision of the job of the music teacher. The student teacher should plan to attend all after-school and weekend music events the co-operating teacher attends. If possible, participate in parent teacher conferences and take the opportunity to interact with the parents. Go to festivals and contests that students perform in even if you are not directly involved.

Music teachers spend a great deal of time and energy on non-music planning and administration of the music program. Try to learn as much as possible about these duties. Be involved in writing report cards, creating the budget, planning a trip, creating the concert program, etc. This may mean that you must adjust your personal schedule for the student teaching semester. The co-operating teacher and the building administrators want to know that you are committed to the job, and assistance and involvement in all aspects of the program are musts.

Other Experiences at the School

There are always days during the student teaching semester when the student teacher may have to arrange his or her own learning because the students are away at a field trip or in testing, or because the co-operating teacher is out. Don't observe the substitute teacher. Your time can be made more meaningful by doing one of the activities listed below. Find time somewhere in the student teaching experience for as many of these activities as possible.

- Observe some of the music students in another classroom (non-music), and note how they interact in this setting.
- Observe another music teacher (maybe even in another district) who teaches the same grade and subject as your co-operating teacher, and compare the teaching approach and strategies.
- Shadow a student for the day to learn more about the rest of the school.
- Observe a teacher in another area of music education (in which you will not student teach). For example, if you are student teaching in band, go observe the choir.
- Interview students about their experiences in music classes.
- Ask the building principal or a district administrator to hold a mock job interview.

A common challenge for student teachers is understanding their own identities. This process continues through student teaching and into the first year. In the story below, Brittany describes how a sixth grade student helped her to see herself as a teacher who is a musician instead of a musician who is a teacher. This transition is common for beginning music teachers. Teachers in other content areas often state that their interest in becoming a teacher centers on a desire to be around children. However, music teachers are often more taken by the desire to be around music. Making the transition from a music-focused music teacher to a student-focused music teacher is important in the growth of the beginning music teacher.

Musician Who Teaches or Teacher Who Is a Musician?

My methods classes, the observations in many districts, and learning correct conducting techniques in college all prepared me for the musical experiences of an orchestra classroom. I went into student teaching believing I was ready to efficiently teach the art and craft of music. Admittedly, my focus was on teaching music merely because I liked music, but thankfully my heart was quickly captured by the sixth, seventh, and eighth graders who have since changed my understanding of teaching. Through my special co-operating teacher and her diverse orchestra program, I finally got it; I saw it happening. Music in this middle school was not just spreading the clichés of music appreciation or the passion and joy of music—it had life-changing effects on individual students.

I first met a particularly eager seventh grade girl during what was called Viking Time. Every morning she would come down to practice or get new music during this extra fifteen minutes of homeroom. She had questions like "Miss Uschold, how do I play this rhythm?" or "Miss Uschold, how do I vibrate on a fourth finger?" but it was not this drive to play well that distinguished her from her peers. This particular student clearly loved playing her violin in orchestra, but her love for orchestra did not stop when class was over. She would hang around before or after school and during her free period to talk, organize, or clean up. The orchestra classroom was her home at school. She felt comfortable and encouraged by my co-operating teacher, who was willing to give of her time, ears, and attention. Although this young musician learned to love music from my co-operating teacher, I discovered that she especially loved the confidence orchestra gave her during these typically self-conscious middle school years.

Although I observed this dynamic interaction from my co-operating teacher, who seemed to easily relate to her growing musicians, I had yet to experience these effects personally. From my third week, I was given free reign to teach the sixth graders, and I loved every one of them. So many curious little gazes and energetic personalities brightened my afternoons; however, one spunky, chatty, and spirited sixth grader was noticeable from my first day. This student was the class cheerleader and the mouthy class clown. She had a unique way of pumping up her peers for the last hour of the day, yet all this masked her own insecurities about her ability to play violin.

I'm not sure how much this student liked to play in class before she was introduced to an arrangement of Pachelbel's Canon in D for orchestra. When faced with a test on the most challenging section of running sixteenth notes, the class was aware that this student in the second violin section was frustrated as she announced, "I do NOT like this piece!" Although she was aggravated, it was natural to encourage her to succeed. We made pacts about practicing at home and worked hard at school together. Now this sixth grader truly can play the piece beautifully because of the combination of support and hard work. And despite the fact that the test has since passed, she still comes down to the classroom during Viking Time to practice. It is my hope that she now feels a sense of pride and empowerment in the realization that she met a difficult challenge. The orchestra classroom is now her encouraging home.

I admit that before these events Pachelbel's Canon in D was one of my least favorite selections, but my spunky sixth grade student gave it renewed meaning. It is amazing how music education touches both the life of the student and of the teacher. I have realized that teaching the music on the page is secondary to meeting the individual needs of students. Such personal impacts were described to me while at the university, but observing music education in action and being a part of it has made it tangible to my heart. I have discovered that I am not a musician who teaches, but I am a teacher who is a musician.

—Brittany Uschold

Questions for Discussion

• Music classrooms offer a unique opportunity for students to grow and learn in schools. Why are music classes often viewed in a different light from "academic" classes?
• In what ways (or with what strategies) can a comforting but motivating classroom be created to provide inspiration for achievement?

Chapter Six
Feedback and Growth
in Student Teaching

During student teaching you have an opportunity to grow as a teacher, as a musician, and as a person. Never again in your teaching career will you have a co-operating teacher or a university supervisor to assist you in your work. Students in the program know that you are a student teacher and often give you a break in a way that they will not once you have your own classroom.

This chapter includes sample student teacher reflection forms that you may use to formulate strategies for improvement and forms for collecting feedback from your students. We would suggest using these forms as guides in developing your own form, which will be more specific to your teaching setting. The exercise of creating the form in itself may serve as a powerful reflection activity prior to your student teaching experience.

The Co-operating Teacher

Although student teaching programs vary a great deal, the role of the co-operating teacher is fairly consistent from program to program. By agreeing to take a student teacher, the co-operating teacher states his or her desire to mentor the next generation of music teachers. Most co-operating teachers really do want the student teacher to be successful. Many institutions send a letter or a handbook to co-operating teachers to clarify their roles. We have included an outline of the most common information in these handbooks so that the student teachers will be aware of the co-operating teacher's likely expectations.

Responsibilities of the Co-operating Teacher

- Prepare your students in the classroom for the arrival of the student teacher. Introduce the student teacher to the class as Mr. or Ms. and treat him or her as a colleague in front of the students.

- Make the student teacher aware of district and building policies and procedures. Share relevant information about students with the student teacher.
- Develop a schedule for the student teaching experience that includes observation in the early days and eventually some teaching duties and ends with a few full days of teaching by the student teacher.
- Provide verbal and written feedback to the student teacher regarding his or her progress.
- Communicate regularly with the university regarding the progress of the student teacher.

The College or University Supervisor

The role of the college supervisor is less standard than the role of the co-operating teacher. Supervisors may be music education professors, education professors, ensemble conductors, retired music teachers, retired teachers, or doctoral students in education or music education. In some programs, the college or university supervisor may come once a week or once every other week. In other settings, the supervisor may come only two or three times each semester; different supervisors may come, and the same person may not see the student teacher more than once. All of this depends on the size of the school, the number of student teachers, and how many supervisors are available for this work. Still, there are some elements of the role that are consistent.

Role of the Supervisor

- Provide verbal and written feedback to the student teacher regarding his or her progress.
- Work as a liaison between the student teacher, the co-operating teacher, and the university.
- Help the student teacher to make the most of the student teaching experience.
- Encourage the student teacher to consider issues of teaching and learning beyond the single context he or she is working in.

Sample Reflection Worksheets for Student Teaching

The most important element of student teaching is learning how to think back on your work and create strategies for improvement. The tools in this section are examples of forms that may be used to facilitate your reflection on student teaching experiences. All three examples have the same basic intent but are provided here so that different student teachers have different options for reflection forms. You may find that a simple journal documenting your daily experiences and providing space for personal comment works for you. The bottom line is to find some way of writing down all of your thoughts, concerns, and questions in this exciting time.

Reflection Worksheet #1 comes from Robert Erbes, Michigan State University; #2 from Herbert Marshall, University of Michigan; and #3 from Louis Bergonzi, developed for the Eastman School of Music.

Reflection Worksheet #1

I spent approximately____ hours in actual teaching this week.

What one or two words best describe your teaching experience this week?

What went well this week?

Did you reach your personal teaching goals this week?

If you had this week to do over again, knowing what you know now, what would you do differently?

What did you do in terms of trying new ideas, concepts, techniques, etc.? How did it pay off in terms of what you and/or your students learned?

Reflection Worksheet #2

Name_____

School_____

Date_____

Brief description of class or learner(s):

What? Describe an interesting occurrence or situation.

So what? Tell why this was significant.

Now what? What course of action will you take, or what have you learned as a result of this event?

Reflection Worksheet #3

Name _____ Date _____

Class_____ School_____ Number of students_____

A. Describe what you noticed about the following aspects of your teaching.

Aspects of Instruction	Comments
Were the objectives clear?	
Was the lesson well organized?	
Did you properly set up the learning environment?	
Was there continuity between activities?	
How well did the students complete your objectives?	
Did you offer assessments after students performed?	
Did you display good posture and a sense of confidence?	

Aspects of Instruction	Comments
Did you maintain eye contact with the entire class?	
Did you display any distracting mannerisms?	
Were your instructions clear?	
Was your voice well projected and understandable?	
Were your musical models of good quality? Were you visual models of good quality?	
How well did you diagnose the problems (visually and aurally)?	
Did you use your singing voice well as a model?	
Did you offer remediation activities for poor student performances?	
How well did the students pay attention?	
Were you aware of the entire classroom?	

B. Describe three aspects of your teaching that you consider strengths, and give at least one specific example from this lesson.

Aspect	Example
1.	
2.	
3.	

C. Describe three aspects of your teaching that you think can be improved, give at least one example from this lesson, and explain how you would do it differently next time.

Aspect	Example(s)	Remediation
1.		
2.		
3.		

D. Additional Comments (Optional):

Sample Supervisor Observation Forms

In many student teaching settings supervisors will use observation forms that are provided by the department or school of education. The forms from the Eastman School of Music, Michigan State University, and the University of Delaware all solicit music-specific information.

Supervisor Observation Form #1 is by Louis Bergonzi, developed for the Eastman School of Music; Form #2 is by Robert Erbes, Michigan State University; Form #3 is by Suzanne Burton, University of Delaware; and Form #4 is by Herbert Marshall, Universtiy of Michigan.

Supervisor Observation Form #1

Student teacher _____Observer _____

Class_____ School _____ Number of students _____

Instructional time _____ Special considerations_____

Length of period _____ Date_____ Observation_____

Instructional Techniques	Comments and Suggestions
I. Introduction to the Lesson Did the instructor establish good initial contact with the class? Were the objectives clear? Was appropriate motivation toward learning evident?	
II. Presentation Was the material well organized? Was the pace of instruction appropriate? Did the instruction have continuity between activities?	

Instructional Techniques	Comments and Suggestions
Were illustrations and examples used to reinforce the material? Were media aids effectively used?	
III. Teaching Procedures Were the activities appropriate for achieving the stated objectives? Were the explanations and demonstrations coordinated? Were the procedures appropriate for the students? Were students provided with supportive assessments? Was the instructor sensitive to individual student differences? Were the closing activities effective?	

Instructional Techniques	Comments and Suggestions
IV. Instructor Qualities and Verbal Fluency Did the instructor possess poise and confidence? Did he or she display a positive attitude? Was the instructor sensitive to the feelings, needs, and interests of the students? Did he or she maintain eye contact? Were there any distracting mannerisms? Was he or she enthusiastic while teaching? Were instructions expressed clearly and fluently? Did the instructor's voice project to all parts of the room?	

Instructional Techniques	Comments and Suggestions
Were the phraseology and usage of English appropriate?	
V. Musical Skills Were the following skills effectively used? • Modeling skills • Visual diagnostic skills • Aural diagnostic skills • Accompaniment skills • Performance skills • Conducting skills • Intonation skills • Use of classroom instruments • Movement Was the singing voice effectively used in instruction? Did the instructor demonstrate comprehensive musicianship?	

Instructional Techniques	Comments and Suggestions
VI. *Classroom Management* Were routine matters properly handled? Were any discipline problems apparent? Did the instructor maintain the awareness of the entire class? Was rule enforcement consistent? Were students engaged in learning? Did the instructor properly plan for student participation? Were students' questions handled with skill?	
VII. *Student Education* Did the class (or the students) achieve the instructional objectives?	

Instructional Techniques	Comments and Suggestions
Were evaluative procedures effectively used?	
What were the level and quality of student responses?	
Were students actively participating in the lesson?	

+ = exceptional; absence of mark does not imply deficiency.

POST CONFERENCE: AREAS OF FOCUS

Strengths:

Recommendations for Improvement: (Follow-up Planned)

_____   _____   _____
Signature of Observer   Signature of Student Teacher   Date

Supervisor Observation Form #2

1 = poor; 2 = fair; 3 = adequate; 4 = good; 5 = excellent; NA = not applicable or not observed.

Subject Matter Skills　　(circle one)

Demonstrates command of subject matter.	1	2	3	4	5	NA
Demonstrates effective conducting skills.	1	2	3	4	5	NA
Demonstrates competency on keyboard, classroom instruments, or secondary instruments.	1	2	3	4	5	NA
Demonstrates effective teaching pedagogy in major field.	1	2	3	4	5	NA
Teaches basic musical concepts effectively.	1	2	3	4	5	NA
Demonstrates effective musicianship.	1	2	3	4	5	NA

Other Comments:

Instructional and Management Skills

Uses effective instructional and/or rehearsal techniques.	1	2	3	4	5	NA
Uses a variety of instructional and rehearsal techniques.	1	2	3	4	5	NA
Considers students' individual needs and abilities.	1	2	3	4	5	NA
Uses effective management skills.	1	2	3	4	5	NA
Develops appropriate class and rehearsal routines.	1	2	3	4	5	NA
Uses appropriate pacing and holds students' interest.	1	2	3	4	5	NA

Other Comments:

Planning, Organizational, and Evaluation Skills

Incorporates students' needs and abilities
in planning.   1   2   3   4   5   NA

Selects appropriate goals and/or objectives.   1   2   3   4   5   NA

Uses effective planning techniques.   1   2   3   4   5   NA

Selects appropriate materials and literature.   1   2   3   4   5   NA

Uses appropriate and effective evaluation
techniques.   1   2   3   4   5   NA

Is personally organized.   1   2   3   4   5   NA

Other Comments:

Interpersonal Relationship Skills

Has rapport with students.   1   2   3   4   5   NA

Has students' respect.   1   2   3   4   5   NA

Has rapport with staff.   1   2   3   4   5   NA

Is cooperative with supervisor(s) and staff.   1   2   3   4   5   NA

Is sensitive to individual learners regardless of
gender, race, or ethnicity.   1   2   3   4   5   NA

Other Comments:

Personal and Professional Qualities

Demonstrates effective verbal communication
skills.   1   2   3   4   5   NA

Demonstrates effective nonverbal communication
skills.   1   2   3   4   5   NA

Demonstrates effective written communication
skills.   1   2   3   4   5   NA

Demonstrates enthusiasm and interest in

teaching.   1   2   3   4   5   NA

Demonstrates creativity in teaching.   1   2   3   4   5   NA

Demonstrates initiative.   1   2   3   4   5   NA

Demonstrates patience and understanding.   1   2   3   4   5   NA

Fulfills obligations, is dependable, and reliable.   1   2   3   4   5   NA

Demonstrates emotional maturity.   1   2   3   4   5   NA

Demonstrates appropriate dress, appearance,

and manner.   1   2   3   4   5   NA

Is capable of evaluating his or her performance.   1   2   3   4   5   NA

Exhibits professional behavior in and out

of school.   1   2   3   4   5   NA

Other Comments:

Supervisor Observation Form #3

Student Teacher_____

Evaluator_____ Date_____

Quality of skills exhibited

1.....................................3.....................................5
Not mastered......................................Highly Effective

Organizes Content Knowledge

Background and needs of the learners are considered.	1	2	3	4	5	NA
Has written and approved lesson plans.	1	2	3	4	5	NA
Addresses state music content standards.	1	2	3	4	5	NA
Learning objectives are appropriate.	1	2	3	4	5	NA
Presentation of content is sequential.	1	2	3	4	5	NA
Planning builds on prior knowledge and learning.	1	2	3	4	5	NA
Teaching methods and techniques align with objectives.	1	2	3	4	5	NA
Assessment aligns with objectives.	1	2	3	4	5	NA
Plans extensions for future learning.	1	2	3	4	5	NA

Creates Effective Learning Environment

Establishes climate that promotes fairness and mutual respect.	1	2	3	4	5	NA
Develops rapport with learners.	1	2	3	4	5	NA
Challenges students toward musical excellence.	1	2	3	4	5	NA

Differentiates instruction to meet individual needs.   1 2 3 4 5 NA

Demonstrates effective and consistent classroom
management skills.   1 2 3 4 5 NA

Creates a safe learning environment.   1 2 3 4 5 NA

Teaches to Accommodate Student Learning
Knows lesson plan.   1 2 3 4 5 NA

Understands content to be presented.   1 2 3 4 5 NA

Presents instruction in a clear and effective manner.   1 2 3 4 5 NA

Presentation of content is sequential and appropriate
for the learning context.   1 2 3 4 5 NA

Encourages students to extend their thinking.   1 2 3 4 5 NA

Adjusts instruction as the situation demands.   1 2 3 4 5 NA

Uses instructional time effectively.   1 2 3 4 5 NA

Musical Presentation
Is a musical model and leader.   1 2 3 4 5 NA

Demonstrates rhythmic accuracy.   1 2 3 4 5 NA

Demonstrates pitch accuracy.   1 2 3 4 5 NA

Identifies musical mistakes aurally and/or
through observation.   1 2 3 4 5 NA

Monitors student learning and provides feedback.   1   2   3   4   5   NA

Prescribes effective and musical solutions.   1   2   3   4   5   NA

Musical solutions meet developmental needs of the
learners.   1   2   3   4   5   NA

Musical progress is evident.   1   2   3   4   5   NA

Demonstrates functional keyboard skills.   1   2   3   4   5   NA

Demonstrates classroom instrument skills.   1   2   3   4   5   NA

General Presentation Skills
Starts lesson on time.   1   2   3   4   5   NA

Ends lesson on time.   1   2   3   4   5   NA

Pacing is appropriate.   1   2   3   4   5   NA

Projects voice.   1   2   3   4   5   NA

Articulates clearly with correct grammar.   1   2   3   4   5   NA

Writes coherently with correct grammar and spelling.   1   2   3   4   5   NA

Demonstrates enthusiasm for teaching music.   1   2   3   4   5   NA

Reflective Practice
Reflects on overall lesson effectiveness.   1   2   3   4   5   NA

Evaluates what was taught and learned.   1   2   3   4   5   NA

Provides evidence of student learning.   1   2   3   4   5   NA

Teacher Professionalism

Demonstrates sense of efficacy.	1	2	3	4	5	NA
Accepts and utilizes constructive criticism.	1	2	3	4	5	NA
Communicates with cooperating teacher.	1	2	3	4	5	NA
Communicates with school community.	1	2	3	4	5	NA
Builds professional relationships.	1	2	3	4	5	NA
Wears appropriate professional attire.	1	2	3	4	5	NA
Takes initiative.	1	2	3	4	5	NA
Is organized.	1	2	3	4	5	NA
Is punctual.	1	2	3	4	5	NA
Manages time and work effectively.	1	2	3	4	5	NA
Demonstrates responsibility.	1	2	3	4	5	NA

Additional Comments:

Supervisor Observation Form #4

Student teacher_____Observer_____

School:_____   Class:_____

Number of students:_____Instructional time:_____ Length of period:_____

Special considerations:_____Date:_____

Instructional Techniques   **Comments and Suggestions**

Introduction to Lesson

1. Did the instructor establish good initial contact with the class?

2. Were the objectives clear?

3. Was appropriate motivation toward learning evident?

Presentation

1. Was the material well organized?

2. Was the pace of instruction appropriate?

3. Did the instruction have continuity between activities?

4. Were illustrations and examples used to reinforce the material?

5. Were media aids effectively used?

Teaching Procedure

1. Was the procedure appropriate for the lesson?

2. Were explanations and demonstrations coordinated?

3. Were the activities appropriate for achieving the stated objectives?

4.   Were students provided with supportive assessments?

5.   Was the instructor sensitive to individual student differences?

6.   Were the closing activities effective?

Instructor Qualities and Verbal Fluency

1.   Did the instructor possess poise and confidence?

2.   Did he or she display a positive attitude?

3.   Was the instructor sensitive to the feelings, needs, and interests of the students?

4.   Did he or she maintain eye contact?

5.   Were there any distracting mannerisms?

6.   Was he or she enthusiastic while teaching?

7.   Were instructions expressed clearly and fluently?

8.   Did the instructor's voice project to all parts of the room?

9.   Was the phraseology and usage of English appropriate?

Musical Skills

1.   Were the following skills used effectively?

Modeling skills

Visual diagnostic skills

Aural diagnostic skills

Accompaniment skills

Performance skills

Conducting skills

Intonation skills

Use of classroom instruments

Movement

2. Was the singing voice effectively use in instruction?

3. Did the instructor demonstrate comprehensive musicianship?

Classroom Management

1. Were routine matters properly handled?

2. Were any discipline problems apparent?

3. Did the instructor maintain awareness of the entire class?

4. Was rule enforcement consistent?

5. Were students engaged in learning?

6. Did the instructor properly plan for student participation?

7. Were student's questions handled with skill?

Student Evaluation

1. Did the class (or students) achieve the instructional objectives?

2. Were evaluation procedures effectively used?

3. What were the level and quality of student responses?

4. Were students actively participating in the lesson?

Sample Student Feedback Forms

Many student teachers find it useful to collect feedback from the P–12 students. Students of any age can tell you how helpful you were to their learning and what you might do to be more helpful. The two forms in this section are provided as examples of what you might design to give to students. Depending on the age of your students and the content of the course, you will need to adjust the forms to your teaching setting. Be sure to go over the forms and the procedures for collecting this information from students with your co-operating teacher.

Student Feedback Form #1 comes from Robert Erbes, Michigan State University, and #2 comes from Herbert Marshall, University of Michigan (with students from Georgia State University).

Student Feedback Form #1

1. How often do I talk in class (giving explanations or instructions)?
    a. Too much
    b. About the right amount
    c. Too little
    d. Does not apply

2. My speaking voice usually is:
    a. Too loud.
    b. Loud enough to be understood clearly.
    c. Too soft.
    d. Does not apply

3. How clear am I in presenting my ideas?
    a. Very clear
    b. Sometimes hazy
    c. Very difficult to understand
    d. Does not apply

4. How often do I go over problems in the music that are hard for you?
    a. Too many times
    b. About the right number of times
    c. Not enough times
    d. Does not apply

5. When rehearsing or teaching various pieces, I tend to:
    a. Stay on one piece too long.
    b. Rehearse a piece about the right length of time.
    c. Skip around too much.
    d. Does not apply

6. Do I make it clear how I want the music to be performed?
    a. Instructions are almost always clear.
    b. Part of the time I am not sure what you want.
    c. Instructions are seldom clear.
    d. Does not apply

7. As a rule, my conducting is:
    a. Very easy to follow.
    b. Fairly easy to follow.
    c. Very hard to follow.
    d. Does not apply

8. How appropriate is my conducting?
    a. Is appropriate
    b. Unclear at times, but usually okay
    c. Is inappropriate
    d. Does not apply

9. How much do I seem to expect of you when it comes to learning and performing music?
    a. Not enough
    b. About the right amount
    c. Too much
    d. Does not apply

10. How would you describe my interest and enthusiasm for this music class?
    a. Excited
    b. Casually interested
    c. Indifferent
    d. Does not apply

11. Do I inspire you to do your best in music?
    a. Very much so
    b. Sometimes
    c. Not at all
    d. Does not apply

12. How much interest do I take in you personally?
    a. A great deal
    b. Some interest
    c. Very little
    d. Does not apply

13. How do you feel about making requests and asking questions of me?
    a. Afraid to request anything
    b. Willing to request something if necessary
    c. Very much at ease in making a request
    d. Does not apply

14. Do you feel I tend to pick on certain students? (This includes both favorable and unfavorable contexts.)
    a. Everyone treated equally
    b. A little bit
    c. Very much so
    d. Does not apply

15. My approach to discipline is:
    a. Too easy.
    b. About right.
    c. Too strict.
    d. Does not apply

16. Do you think that as a teacher I should be firmer or less firm?
    a. Be firmer.
    b. Be about the same.
    c. Be less firm.
    d. Does not apply

17. Do I appear prepared for each class?

    a. You seem very well prepared and organized.

    b. You seem to be somewhat prepared.

    c. You seem to start class with no idea of what to do.

    d. Does not apply

18. How did you like the music I selected?
    a. Liked it all a lot
    b. It was mostly okay.
    c. It was not that interesting to me.
    d. Does not apply

If you have other suggestions, please write them below.

Student Feedback Form #2

Your answers to these few questions will help me improve as a music teacher. Please read the numbered statements and indicate how often that statement was true about my teaching by circling: never, a few times, about half the time, most of the time, or always. Do your best to circle the best answer for each without changing anything. Then use the open questions at the end to write additional advice you feel is important for me to know.

1. When the student teacher was in charge of the class, I knew I was learning something about music.

    never   a few times   about half the time   most of the time   always

2. While teaching, the student teacher behaves as maturely and professionally as most of the good teachers in this school.

    never   a few times   about half the time   most of the time   always

3. When asked serious questions, the student teacher knew or could find out a good answer.

    never   a few times   about half the time   most of the time   always

4. I could tell that the student teacher knew a lot about music.

    never   a few times   about half the time   most of the time   always

5. I was comfortable asking the student teacher questions about music.

    never   a few times   about half the time   most of the time   always

6. This student teacher was someone I felt I could talk to about a problem (musical or not).

    never   a few times   about half the time   most of the time   always

7. During class, the student teacher treated everyone fairly.

    never   a few times   about half the time   most of the time   always

8. I feel the student teacher treated me with respect.

    never   a few times   about half the time   most of the time   always

9. I feel the student teacher treated our class with respect.

   never   a few times   about half the time   most of the time   always

10. When the student teacher was in charge, class began on time.

    never   a few times   about half the time   most of the time   always

11. While the student teacher was teaching, I felt my regular music teacher could leave the room and everything would keep going like normal.

    never   a few times   about half the time   most of the time   always

12. While teaching, the student teacher showed me that he or she was ready to be a full-time teacher.

    never   a few times   about half the time   most of the time   always

13. While the student teacher was teaching, I wasn't learning anything about music.

    never   a few times   about half the time   most of the time   always

14. The way the student teacher taught made it difficult to learn music.

    never   a few times   about half the time   most of the time   always

15. While the student teacher was teaching, I enjoyed learning.

    never   a few times   about half the time   most of the time   always

16. During music class with the student teacher, I felt like I needed him or her to talk and explain more, rather than participating and making music.

    never   a few times   about half the time   most of the time   always

17. During music class with the student teacher, I felt like I needed more participation and music making rather than more talking and explanation.

    never   a few times   about half the time   most of the time   always

18. I felt like I couldn't or shouldn't ask the student teacher questions about music.

    never   a few times   about half the time   most of the time   always

19. The student teacher seemed unsure about how to answer questions about music.

    never   a few times   about half the time   most of the time   always

20. The student teacher was disrespectful and rude in class.

    never   a few times   about half the time   most of the time   always

21. There was a clear sense of teamwork when the student teacher was working with my regular music teacher(s).

    never   a few times   about half the time   most of the time   always

22. In class or rehearsal the student teacher gave clear instructions. I knew what I was supposed to do.

    never   a few times   about half the time   most of the time   always

23. The student teacher seemed confident and in control while teaching the class.

    never   a few times   about half the time   most of the time   always

24. The student teacher seemed to have lower expectations for us than our regular teacher.

    never   a few times   about half the time   most of the time   always

25. The student teacher seemed to have higher expectations for us than our regular teacher.

    never   a few times   about half the time   most of the time   always

26. During his or her time with us, I could tell the student teacher loved music.

    never   a few times   about half the time   most of the time   always

27. During his or her time with us, I could tell the student teacher loved teaching.

    never   a few times   about half the time   most of the time   always

Please write about the strengths of the student teacher—the things to keep doing well.

Please write about the weaknesses of the student teacher—the things that need improving.

Chapter Seven
Student Teaching Seminar

In most institutions student teachers are expected to return to campus for a student teaching seminar course. These seminars vary from meetings just a few times each semester to meetings several times in a week. In smaller schools, music students may attend the seminar with teacher education students from other content areas, whereas in larger schools the seminar may be for music student teachers only. The purpose of this chapter is to examine some of the most common discussion topics for student teaching seminar and provide discussion cases and/or suggested activities and resources for the seminar format.

One of the most valuable aspects of student teaching seminar is the opportunity to hear about the experiences of student teachers in other settings. Even in seminars where many of the other students are in content areas other than music you can learn a great deal about classroom management, working with parents, planning for instruction, and general work in schools. Other typical seminar topics include the job search, writing a cover letter, preparing a resume and teaching portfolio, interviewing for a job, meeting the challenges faced by beginning music teachers, mentoring, and professional development. These other topics are addressed in Chapters Eight through Twelve.

Classroom Management

Student teachers in music regularly struggle with issues of classroom management. (First-year teachers have problems with it as well, which are addressed again in Chapter Nine.) It is important for the student teacher to model the classroom management strategies used by the co-operating teacher even if he or she does not agree with the strategies. During the first few days of observation, focus special attention on the classroom management strategies. If there are no classroom management issues (e.g., discipline problems) in the class this probably means there are lots of behind the scenes management strategies that keep things running smoothly. Learn how to set them up for future reference.

Be careful not to end up in the middle of issues between students and the co-operating teacher. Music students are often like children who ask one parent for something, and when they are told "no" they go to the other parent and ask for the same thing. Always support the co-operating teacher, and you have a better chance that the co-operating teacher will do the same. Do not allow students to come to you to complain about the co-operating teacher. Be sure you understand the classroom rules and insist that students adhere to them. If you think that there should be more rules, discuss possible changes in classroom management policy with the co-operating teacher before implementing new ideas with students. I always tell my student to use the university as an excuse for trying something new. You might say to the co-operating teacher: "In our seminar last week we discussed classroom management, and it was suggested that we experiment with a 'no play' rule at the beginning of class in instrumental ensembles."

Reflective teachers always ask themselves how they could change in order to best meet the needs of students. Even with regard to student behavior, the teacher must look at how he or she can change. You will hear teachers in the teachers' lounge discussing "these kids" or "this class."

It is true that some groups of students are more challenging than others. However, it is always the job of the teacher to continue to explore new strategies for teaching.

Suggested activity: Read the classroom management cases in Chapter Nine, and discuss the questions with your peers. Although the cases are placed within the context of first-year teaching and not student teaching, many of the strategies modeled would work in other types of music classrooms.

Classroom Management—
Suggestions for Further Reading and Discussion

Bartholomew, D. 1993. Effective strategies for praising students. *Music Educators Journal* 80(3): 40–43.

Barrow, L. G. 1994. Programming rehearsals for student success. *Music Educators Journal* 81(2): 26–28

Buck, G. H. 1992. Classroom management and the disruptive child. *Music Educators Journal* 70(3): 36–42.

Eshelman, D., and J. Nelson. 1994. A teacher's guide to first-year survival. *Music Educators Journal* 81(1): 29–31, 47.

Gumm, A. J. 1994. Music teaching style ideas and implications. *Music Educators Journal* 80(4): 33–36.

Madsen, C. H., and C. K. Madsen. 1981. *Teaching/discipline: A positive approach for educational development.* Boston: Allyn and Bacon, Inc.

Merrion, M. 1990. How master teachers handle discipline. *Music Educators Journal* 77(2): 26–29.

———. 1991. Classroom management for beginning music educators. *Music Educators Journal* 70(2): 53–56.

Music Educators National Conference. 2004. *Spotlight on transition to teaching music.* Reston, VA: MENC.

Nimmo, D. 1997. Judicious discipline in the music classroom. *Music Educators Journal* 83(4): 27–32.

Snyder, D. W. 1998. Classroom management for student teachers. *Music Educators Journal* 84(4): 37–40.

Stufft, W. D. 1997. Two rules for professional conduct. *Music Educators Journal* 84(1): 40–42.

Walker, D. E. 1993. A survival kit for new music teachers. *Music Educators Journal* 80(2): 27–29.

Wignes, G. 1995. Strategies to improve student response. *Music Educators Journal* 81(4): 27–32.

Lesson Planning and Curriculum Design

When you do begin to teach, you may find that the style of planning for lessons you learned in your teacher education program does not match the style used by your co-operating teacher. Many experienced music teachers no longer write lesson plans as you might think of them. They have given some of their lessons so many times that they no longer need to write down their ideas. However, research has suggested that young teachers still need to write specific plans for classes. It is sometimes difficult to get the co-operating teacher to tell you in advance of a lesson or day what you will be doing. Student teachers must be carefully proactive with the co-operating teachers in reminding them that they need some time to plan for good lessons.

We have found that in addition to planning the musical material for a lesson that many of our students benefit from planning the questions they will ask students and how they will articulate certain concepts—almost writing a "script" for the lesson that includes specific questions to ask students. Otherwise, young teachers often do most of the talking and all of the musical decision making. Think about what you might say to the students or tell them, and then see if there is a way to phrase a question that gets the students to generate that same information.

Most of the lessons you design will be based on the curriculum put together by the co-operating teacher. Sometimes this means that you must teach something you are unfamiliar with or must present it in a way with which you do not agree. Remember, the classroom is really not your classroom. It is perfectly appropriate later on in the semester to discuss the incorporation of your own ideas into the lesson plans. However, the student teacher must respect that the co-operating teacher may not want to try something unfamiliar when you are leaving in just a few weeks.

Suggested activities: (1) Gather curriculum documents from your co-operating teacher, and compare what you have gathered with the curriculum materials from other students in the class. (2) Search the Web for the state music frameworks in the state where you are interested in teaching. Bring these to class, and compare them with state frameworks from other states. (3) Read the case "In Search of the Curriculum" in Chapter Ten and review the discussion questions.

Lesson Planning and Curriculum— Suggestions for Further Reading and Discussion

General Curriculum

Apple, M. W. 1996. *Cultural politics and education*. New York: Teachers College Press.

Bruner, J. 1960. *The process of education*. Cambridge: Harvard University Press.

Connelly, F. M., and D. J. Clandinin. 1988. *Teachers as curriculum planners: Narratives of experience*. New York: Teachers College Press.

Dewey, J. 1916. *Democracy and education*. New York: Macmillan.

———. 1938. *Experience and education*. New York: Macmillan.

Doll, W. E. 1993. *A post-modern perspective on curriculum*. New York: Teachers College Press.

Eisner, E. 1994. *The educational imagination: On the design and evaluation of school programs*. 3rd ed. New York: Macmillan.

Freire, P. 1970. *Pedagogy of the oppressed*. New York: Herder and Herder.

Kleibard, H. 1987. *The struggle for the American curriculum 1893–1958*. London: Routledge and Kegan Paul.

Slattery, P. 1995. *Curriculum development in the postmodern era*. New York: Garland Publishers.

Tyler, R. W. 1949. *Basic principles of curriculum and instruction*. Chicago: University of Chicago Press.

Walker, D. F., and J. F. Soltis. 2004. *Curriculum and aims*. 4th ed. New York: Teachers College Press. (See also Conway, C. M.)

Wiles, J. 1999. *Curriculum essentials: A resource for educators*. Boston: Allyn and Bacon.

Whitehead, A. N. 1929. *The aims of education*. New York: The Free Press.

Music Curriculum

Abeles, H. F., C. R. Hoffer, and R. H. Klotman. 1994. *Foundations of music education*. 2nd ed. New York: Schirmer Books, 303–341.

Conway, C. M. 2002. Curriculum writing in music. *Music Educators Journal* 88(6): 54–59.

Elliott, D. J. 1995. *Music matters*. New York: Oxford University Press, 241–295.

Hanley, B., and J. Montgomery. 2002. Contemporary curriculum practices and their theoretical bases. In *The New Handbook of Music Teaching and Learning*, ed. R. Colwell and C. Richardson, 113–143. New York: Oxford University Press.

Jorgensen, E. R. 2002. Philosophical issues in curriculum. In *The New Handbook of Music Teaching and Learning*, ed. R. Rolwell and C. Richardson, 48–62. New York: Oxford University Press.

Labuta, J. A., and D. A. Smith. 1997. *Music education: Historical contexts and perspectives*. Upper Saddle River, NJ: Prentice-Hall (curriculum references on 57–68).

Music Educators National Conference. 2005. Special focus – Reconceptualizing curriculum. *Music Educators Journal* 91(4).

Reynolds, H. R. 2000. Repertoire is the curriculum. *Music Educators Journal* 87(1): 31–33.

Wing, L. B. 1992. Curriculum and its study. In *Handbook of research on music teaching and learning*, ed. R. Colwell, 196–217. New York: Schirmer Books.

Assessment of Student Learning

Research on beginning teachers in general education has suggested that grading and assessment are key challenges. Music teachers often have an even greater challenge because they tend to see a large number of students per day. Music teachers who work with volunteer ensembles have to carefully balance providing students and parents with accurate information about musical development while keeping students in music classes and ensembles. Most music teachers struggle with issues of assessment throughout their careers. Recent educational policy (No Child Left Behind) has brought issues of assessment and accountability for student achievement to the forefront for teachers in all subject areas. Although you may not be involved in the grading procedures for students during your student teaching, take the opportunity to learn about these issues during student teaching so you will be prepared in your first year. The activities in this section are designed to get you to consider the many issues connected to good assessment in music classes.

Suggested activity: The case of Mrs. Lowell presented below is a story of a real teacher that was collected through research (The Development of a Casebook for Instrumental Music Education Methods Courses *by Colleen M. Conway, unpublished doctoral dissertation).*

A, B, or C?

Mrs. Lowell has a carefully organized system for grading elementary instrumental music students, which includes encouraging students to evaluate themselves and asking for parent signatures regarding work done at home. At the end of every weekly lesson, Mrs. Lowell and the student look over the student's lesson practice record, discuss how well the student performed at the lesson, and decide together on a grade for the week. The student is supposed to practice at home, and parents sign the practice record each week. In talking about this procedure, Mrs. Lowell says: "Of course, there are times when the parents are either not paying attention or simply not telling the truth. I can tell if the student practiced based on how he sight-read something the week before. So if he comes back and plays exactly the same as last week, I know he has not practiced."

Mrs. Lowell adds, "When it comes time for report cards, the students and I look back at the record to talk about their progress. I bring the report cards to lessons, and the students grade themselves. We consider their progress in reading notation, posture, tone quality, technique, and general knowledge of musical concepts. The students usually decide on the same grade I would give them without the discussion, but I think it's important for them to do this self-evaluation."

Questions for Discussion

- What criteria do you think should be considered when grading students in various music classes? How will you determine grades when you become a teacher?
- What should be done with a student who is working very hard but is still not achieving? What criteria should be considered when grading this type of student?
- It takes time to engage students in conversation regarding their grades. Why does Mrs. Lowell do this? Wouldn't it be faster just to give the students a grade? What is the advantage of student participation in grading?

- How does your co-operating teacher determine grades?
- If a teacher knows student aptitude scores, how should he or she use that information in relation to grading? Should that information be used at all? Discuss your understanding of musical aptitude as it differs from musical achievement.
- Consider and discuss the potential conflict between grading and music course enrollment in secondary ensembles.

Assessment—
Suggestions for Further Reading and Discussion

Arts Propel. www.pz.harvard.edu/research/propel.htm.

Asmus, E. P. 1999. Music assessment concepts. *Music Educators Journal* 86(2): 19–24.

Blocher, L. 1997. The assessment of student learning in band. In *Teaching music through performance in band*, ed. Richard Miles, 27–30. Chicago: GIA Publications.

Boyle, J. D., and R. E. Radocy. 1987. *Measurement and evaluation of musical experiences.* New York: Schirmer Books.

Brophy, T. 1997. Reporting progress with developmental profiles. *Music Educators Journal* 84(1): 26.

Burrack, F. (2002). Enhanced assessment in instrumental programs. *Music Educators Journal* 88(6): 27–32.

Byo, J. L. 2001. Designing substantive playing tests—a model. *Music Educators Journal* 88(2): 39–44.

Chiodo, P. 2001. Assessing a cast of thousands. *Music Educators Journal* 87(6): 17–23.

Cope, C. O. 1996. Steps toward effective assessment. *Music Educators Journal* 83(1): 39–42.

Music Educators National Conference. 1996. *Performance standards for music: Strategies and benchmarks for assessing progress toward the National Standards.* Reston, VA: MENC.

———. 1998. Grading practices in music. *Music Educators Journal* 84(5): 37–40.

———. 1998. The student's role in the assessment process and Making the grade: Authentic assessment in music, K–8. *Teaching Music* 6(2): 32–35, 48.

———. 2001. *Spotlight on assessment.* Reston, VA: MENC.

———. 2003. *Benchmarks in action: A guide to standards-based assessment in music.* Reston, VA: MENC.

Nutter, K. 1999. Managing assessment. *Teaching Music* 7(1): 26–31, 59.

Robinson, M. 1995. Alternative assessment techniques for teachers. *Music Educators Journal* 81(5): 28.

Whitcomb, R. 1999. Writing rubrics for the music classroom. *Music Educators Journal* 86(2): 26–32.

Winner, E., L. Davidson, and L. Scripp. 1992. *Arts PROPEL: A music handbook*. Cambridge: Harvard University Press.

Wolf, D. P., and N. Pistone. 1995. *Taking full measure: Rethinking assessment through the arts*. New York: College Entrance Examination Board.

Motivation

We have listed the topic of motivation here as a separate study topic for the student teaching seminar. However, it is our thought that motivation is carefully connected to all of the other topics (classroom management, lesson planning, curriculum, and assessment). It is not possible to consider motivation for learning separate from those other ideas. It is difficult in a student teaching setting to really have a sense of what motivates students in a classroom because the development of motivation takes longer than a fifteen-week semester. However, it is important for the student teacher to consider the long-term implications of various issues in motivation. The activities in this section are meant to focus the student teaching seminar on these implications.

Suggested activity: The cases of Ms. Rosen and Mr. Greene were developed through research for The Development of a Casebook for Instrumental Music Education Methods Courses *by Colleen M. Conway. Read and respond to both cases.*

Ms. Rosen

In Ms. Rosen's setting, competition is a big motivator because the wind ensemble is a select group chosen by audition. Getting into the wind ensemble is a strong motivator for many of these students. In addition, by the time they get to high school many of them are studying privately and are extremely self-motivated. In order to keep these students excited and challenged, Ms. Rosen must plan her year carefully.

In order to maintain the students' high level of motivation, Ms. Rosen chooses music that is technically and musically challenging for the group. She prepares her musical scores very carefully and expects the students to do the same. The students compete in a state evaluation festival each year and take pride in receiving a high festival rating. For students who are particularly serious about music Ms. Rosen has started an after-school chamber winds ensemble to challenge students on a more advanced level. This group provides additional motivation for its participants.

Ms. Rosen finds the issue of motivation in the symphonic band to be more of a challenge than it is in the wind ensemble. Students in the symphonic band are less self-motivated, less competitive, and less confident about their musical skills than the students in the wind ensemble. In talking about the issue of motivation, Ms. Rosen says, "We work really hard to make students in both bands feel pride in their work. That, I think, is the best motivator."

It is sometimes difficult to build pride in the symphonic band because no matter how well they perform the wind ensemble is always going to be better. Ms. Rosen tries to choose literature for the symphonic band that will be motivating for these students as well. In addition, the symphonic band performs at a state evaluation festival each year, which gives them something to work toward as a group.

Questions for Discussion

- What are your views regarding ability grouping in secondary ensembles?
- Discuss the advantages and disadvantages of using festival and contest participation as motivators.
- How does the relationship between motivation and literature choice change for Ms. Rosen with regard to her different ensembles?
- How does a teacher work to motivate a group like Ms. Rosen's symphonic band?

Mr. Green

Mr. Green works with 150 seventh and eighth grade band students in lessons and ensembles in a large, suburban middle school in upstate New York. He comments that one of the most difficult aspects of his job is that "you get some kids who are forced to stay in band because their parents won't let them quit." Although his program loses only a few students from the program each year, knowing how to deal with a student who thinks he or she wants to quit can really be a challenge.

In discussing his procedures for working with all students, Mr. Green says, "We try to get our students to play better, but we don't beat them up. We understand that these kids have a lot of other things they are doing. We have to deal with reality here. The elementary teacher is trying to send me kids who can play, and I'm trying to do the same for the guy at the high school, but these kids do have lots of other interests. In order to be successful with middle school kids, you have to recognize their limitations."

Mr. Green thinks that dealing with students who may want to quit is important in middle school because back in the elementary school students are just getting started. Instrumental music is still a novelty to them. Elementary students are not as apt to want to quit band. On the other end of the school cycle, if students stay in the program until high school, they are usually fairly committed. Mr. Green says, "The hardest thing about dealing with the quitters is that you really have to treat each situation differently. Depending on the kid, I deal with this in various ways. Sometimes, I say, 'you don't have to be here; there are other options.' If students say that their parents will not let them quit, then I do tell them that if they're here then they have to do the work. Sometimes I get into it with the parents, but not usually. That's awkward. I try not to make a big deal out of dropping for anybody."

Mr. Green shared a specific quitting case—the case of Diana. Diana was the only bassoon student in the eighth grade concert band (the more advanced of the two middle school bands). Diana took private lessons and played quite well. She was usually prepared for lessons and well behaved, although lately she had been disrespectful to Mr. Green on a few occasions (e.g., talking in band, running into lessons at the last possible second and not apologizing for being late, talking in a "wise" way in the hallways within earshot of Mr. Green, etc.). One day after band, Diana asked to talk to Mr. Green for a few minutes:

DIANA: I just wanted to tell you that I'm not going to be in band starting next week. I don't really like it. So, I'm out of here.

MR. GREEN: Have you talked to your parents about this?

DIANA: Yeah, my mom doesn't care. She says, do whatever I want. I'll keep taking lessons so I'll still play, just not in the band. (*Before Mr. Green proceeds he has some careful decisions to make. He says that it's always hard when dealing with a student who plays an instrument that you really need in the band: "Obviously, I did not want to lose my only bassoon in the eighth grade band. However, with the attitude that she was displaying, I didn't really want to tell her how much we needed her. I wasn't sure where her parents were coming from either.*")

MR. GREEN: Well, Diana it's not quite as simple as just quitting whenever you want. You committed to being in this group for the year, and if that is going to change we will need to have a conference between your guidance counselor, your parents, you, and me. Before I set that up can you tell me your reasons for quitting?

DIANA: Well, I just don't like it.

MR. GREEN: What is it that you don't like? You don't like playing the bassoon anymore?

DIANA: No. Like I said, I'm going to keep taking lessons and just not be in the band.

MR. GREEN: Are you still planning to go to solo festival?

DIANA: Yeah, I'm hoping to make All-County again this year.

MR. GREEN: Did you know that you can't be in an All-County group unless you're in your school band?

DIANA: You're kidding, right?

MR. GREEN: No. I'm afraid not. That's a county rule. Maybe we can figure out what it is that you don't like about band and do something about it. If you're not in band, what class will you go to?

DIANA: Well, I'll get to go to study hall and hang out with my friends. I never get to see them.

MR. GREEN: Aren't most of your friends in band?

DIANA: Well, most, but not all. The other thing is, like, all my friends that are in the band play clarinet, and I never even get to see them ever. I sit next to the trombones in band, and then I just have this private lesson. They're always talking about how fun their lessons are and stuff, and I just don't like mine, so I'm gonna quit.

MR. GREEN: Let's consider a compromise. I would be willing to consider moving you to a different place in band, and I'd also be willing to put you in a lesson group with the clarinets and some bass clarinets. However, there are some things I'd need from you in return. Do you want to discuss it?

DIANA: Okay.

MR. GREEN: Well, if I move your seat in band and I have any trouble with you as far as behavior goes—I move you right back—make sense?

DIANA: Yeah.

MR. GREEN: AND, I need you to work on your attitude. No more talking back. I'll do my part to make you like the band situation better if you'll do your part. What do you think?

DIANA: All right. When do I get to change lessons?

Questions for Discussion

- What do you think Mr. Green means when he says that to be successful with middle school students a teacher must "recognize the students' limitations"?
- Mr. Green says that he tries not to "make a big deal" about quitting. What is it that enables him to be fairly relaxed about this issue? Can you think of a different context where students quitting would be a bigger deal?
- How did Mr. Green get Diana to start talking about what she was unhappy with in band?
- What do you think about the compromise made by Mr. Green with Diana? What could the repercussions of this arrangement be?
- Discuss the relationship between this case and the topics of motivation and grading.
- What will you do if there is a student who wants to quit and this is a student you do not particularly care for? Discuss issues associated with liking some students and not liking others.

Motivation—
Suggestions for Further Reading and Discussion

Ames, C., and R. Ames, eds. 1984. *Research on motivation in education.* San Diego: Academic Press.

Asmus, E. P. 1989. The effect of music teachers on students' motivation to achieve in music. *Canadian Journal of Research in Music Education* 30: 14–21.

Austin, J. A. 1991. Competitive and non-competitive goal structures: An analysis of motivation and achievement among elementary band students. *Psychology of Music* 19: 142–158.

Austin, J. A., and W. P. Vispoel. 1998. How American adolescents interpret success and failure in classroom music: Relationships among attributional beliefs, self-concept, and achievement. *Psychology of Music* 26: 26–45.

Eccles, J. S. 1983. Children's motivation to study music. In *Ann Arbor Symposium III on the Application of Psychology to Music Teaching and Learning: Motivation and Creativity.* Reston, VA: MENC.

Fant, G. 1995. Motivational ideas for the musical ensemble. *Music Educators Journal* 81(5): 17–20.

Leenman, T. E. 1995. Keeping beginners in band. *Teaching Music*, 2(6): 24–25, 56.

Madsen, C., R. Greer, and C. Madsen Jr., eds. 1975. *Research in music behavior: Modifying music behavior in the classroom*. New York: Teachers College Press.

Maehr, M., and L. Braskamp. 1986. *The motivation factor*. Lexington, MA: Lexington Books.

Merrion, M., ed. 1989. *What works: Instructional strategies for music education*. Reston, VA: MENC.

Raynor, J. 1981. Motivational determinants of music-related behavior: Psychological careers of student, teacher, performer, and listener. In *Documentary Report of the Ann Arbor Symposium*, 332–351. Reston, VA: MENC.

Thomas, N. G. 1992. Motivation. In *The Handbook of research on music teaching and learning*, ed. R. Colwell, 425–436. New York: Schirmer Books.

Certification Practices

The final topic in this chapter covers certification practices throughout the country. If you are planning to teach in the state where you are a student, this information may not be relevant. However, if you are planning to move out of state, we believe you will find the information in this reprinted figure from the *Journal of Music Teacher Education* to be invaluable. Certification practices change quite regularly so it is recommended that students check with the state education Web site for the most up-to-date information regarding certification practices.

Certification Practices for Music Educators in the Fifty States

State	Certificate Age Levels and Subject Areas	Levels and Length of Certification	Testing Requirements	Reciprocity	Alternative Degree Programs	Fees	Online Forms
Alabama	K–6, 1–9 General K–12 Chorus, Band	5-year Certificate	None	Yes, for comparable certificates	Yes	$20 application $49 fingerprinting	Yes
Alaska	K–6, K–8, 7–12 K–12 Music	5-year Type A	PPST or CBT (basic skills), Alaskan Studies course, Multicultural Education	Yes, 3-year certificate issued while testing and course work are completed	Yes	$90 certificate $66 fingerprinting	Yes
Arizona	K–12, 7–12 Music All level endorsement available	2-year Provisional 6-year Standard	AEPA (professional and content area), US and Arizona constitution class	Yes, 1-year certificate issued while testing and course work is completed	Yes, but not available	$30 certificate $20 renewal	Yes
Arkansas	PreK–8, 7–12, Vocal PreK–8, 7–12 Instrumental	3-year Initial 5-year License	PRAXIS I (basic skills), PLT (professional), PRAXIS II (content area)	Yes, exams can be waived with equivalent tests	Yes	$39 fingerprinting	Yes
California	PreK–12 Music	5-year Preliminary 5-year Professional Clear	CBEST (basic skills), PRAXIS II (content area)	No, CBEST is required, subject area waived with 3+ years experience	Yes	$55 credential $56 fingerprinting	Yes
Colorado	K–12 Music	3-year Provisional 5-year Professional	PLACE (content area)	Yes, exam waived with 3+ years experience	Yes	$48 license $36 fingerprinting	Yes
Connecticut	PreK–12 Music	3-year Initial 8-year Provisional 5-year Professional	CBT (basic skills), PRAXIS II (content area)	Yes, but exams are required	Yes	$50 application $100 initial ($50 credit) $200 Provisional $300 Professional	Support Materials
Delaware	K–8, 5–12 K–12 Music	5-year Standard 5-year Professional	PPST or CBT	Yes, but requires testing	No	No charge in-state $10 out-of-state	Yes
Florida	K–12 Music	5-year Professional	CLAST (basic skills), FPET (professional, FSAE (content area)	Yes, exams can be waived with equivalent tests	Yes	$56 per subject	Yes
Georgia	PreK–12 Music	1-year Conditional (out-of-state) 5-year Clear Renewable	PPST or CBT (basic skills), PRAXIS II (content area)	Yes, other content exams accepted if required	Yes	No charge in state $20 out-of-state	Yes
Hawaii	K–6, 7–12, K–12 Music	5-year Provisional	PPST or CBT (basic skills), PLT (professional), PRAXIS II (content area)	Yes, but testing is required	Yes	No charge	Yes
Idaho	6–12, K–12 Music	5-year Standard Secondary	None	Yes, within the last 5 years	Yes	$35 application $40 fingerprinting	Yes
Illinois	K–9, K–12 Music 5–12 Vocal, Instr.	4-year Initial 5-year Standard	ILCTS (basic skills and content area)	Yes, but test is required	Yes	$30 certificate	Yes

Certification Practices for Music Educators in the Fifty States							
State	Certificate Age Levels and Subject Areas	Levels and Length of Certification	Testing Requirements	Reciprocity	Alternative Degree Programs	Fees	Online Forms
Indiana	Vocal/General/or Instrumental General (Preschool/Elementary, Primary/Elementary, Intermediate, Middle/Junior, and High School)	5-year Initial Practitioner; 10-year Proficient Practitioner; 5-year Accomplished Practitioner	PPST or CBT (basic skills), PRAXIS II (content area)	No, full review of credentials is required	Yes	$5 for each school setting	Yes
Iowa	K–8, 7–12 Music	2-year Initial 5-year Standard	PLT (professional), PRAXIS II (content area)	Yes, 2-year regional exchange license	No	$50 transcript evaluation $50 license $37 fingerprinting	Yes
Kansas	7–12, K–12 Music	3-year/5-year Standard	PLT (professional)	Yes, valid out-of-state receives a 2-year license	Yes	$24 application	No
Kentucky	K–12 Music	5-year Statement of Eligibility; 5-year Provisional	PLT (professional), PRAXIS II (content area)	Yes, exam waived with 2+ years experience	Yes	$35 statement fee $50 provisional	No
Louisiana	1–12 Vocal 1–12 Instrumental	3-year Type C, Lifetime Type B, Lifetime Type A	CBT (basic skills), PLT (professional), PRAXIS II (content area)	3-year provisional while PRAXIS testing is completed	Yes	$55 certificate	Yes
Maine	K–12 Music	2-year Provisional, 5-year Professional	PPST or CBT (basic skills)	Yes	No	$50 certificate	No
Maryland	Nursery–12 Music	3-year Standard I 7-year Standard II 5-year Advanced	PPST or CBT (basic skills), PRAXIS II (content area)	Yes, PPST waived with 3+ years experience	Yes	$10 certificate	No
Massachusetts	PreK–9, 5–12 Vocal, Instrumental, or Composite	5-year Provisional with adv. standing, 5-year Standard master's req.)	MET (basic skills and content area)	Yes, but test is required, 3-year certificate issued while deficiencies are met	No	$100 for first certificate $25 for endorsement (for all level music)	Yes
Michigan	K–5, K–8, 7–12 Music	6-year Provisional 5-year Professional	MTTC (basic skills, professional, content area if secondary	Yes, testing is required but full certification may exempt from testing	Yes	$175 Provisional $125 Professional	Yes
Minnesota	K–12 Vocal/Class, K–12 Instrumental/Class	5-year Professional	PPST or CBT (basic skills), PLT (professional), PRAXIS II (content area), Human Relations Program	No	No	$47 application $26 fingerprinting	Yes
Mississippi	K–12 Vocal/Instrumental	5-year Class A 5-year Class AA	PLT (professional), PRAXIS II (content area)	Yes, 2+ years experience Full, –2 years Special	Yes, but ending	None	Yes
Missouri	K–12 Vocal/Instrumental, endorsement available	3-year PC I 7-year PC II 10-year CPC	PRAXIS II (content area)	Not full, testing is required unless 2+ years experience with other content area test	Yes	No charge in-state $25 out-of-state $22 fingerprinting	Out-of-state only
Montana	K–8, 5–12, 7–12, K–12 Music	Provisional, 5-year Class 2 Standard, 5-year Class 1, Professional	PPST or CBT (basic skills)	Yes, other state basic skills tests accepted	Yes	$6 initial application $6 per year of certificate	Yes

158

Certification Practices for Music Educators in the Fifty States

State	Certificate Age Levels and Subject Areas	Levels and Length of Certification	Testing Requirements	Reciprocity	Alternative Degree Programs	Fees	Online Forms
Nebraska	K–12 Music	5-year Initial 7-year Standard	PPST or CBT (basic skills)	Yes, other state basic skills tests accepted	No	$45 certificate $40 fingerprinting	Yes
Nevada	7–12 Choral, Instrumental, 7–12, K–12 Composite	5-year Standard 6-, 7-, or 10-year Professional	PPST or CBT (basic skills), PLT (professional), PRAXIS II (content area)	Yes, requires courses in US and Nevada constitutions	No	$100 initial application	Yes
New Hampshire	K–12 Music	3-year Beginning Educator, 3-year Experienced Educator	PPST or CBT (basic skills)	Yes, other state basic skills tests accepted	Yes	$80 beginning or renewal	Yes
New Jersey	Nursery–12 Music	Standard Lifetime	PRAXIS II (content area)	Yes, test and 2.75 GPA required	Yes	$10 cert. of eligibility $50 lifetime certificate	No
New Mexico	K–8, 7–12, K–12 Music	3-year Level 1, 9-year Level 2, 9-year Level 3 with master's	NMTA (basic skills and professional)	Yes, other state basic skills and professional tests accepted	Yes	$50 licensure $34 fingerprinting	Yes
New York	PreK–12 Music	5-year Provisional Lifetime Permanent	NYSTCE (basic skills, content area professional)	Yes, but tests required	Yes	$100 certification	Yes
North Carolina	K–12 Music	5-year Continuing	PRAXIS II (content area)	Yes, but tests required	Yes	$85 processing	Yes
North Dakota	K–12 Vocal, Instrumental, Composite	2-year Initial 5-year Professional	North Dakota Native American Studies Course	All credentials must be submitted for review, Native American course is required	No	$25 application packet $60 application $175 out-of-state review $42 fingerprinting	Renewal forms
Ohio	PreK–Music	2-year Provisional 5-year Professional	PLT (professional), PRAXIS II (content area)	Yes, tests may be required depending on original certification date	Yes	$24 provisional $60 professional $50 out-of-state evaluation	No
Oklahoma	PreK–12 Vocal, Instrumental	optional 1-year Provisional, 5-year Certificate	OGET (basic skills), OPTE (professional), OSAT (content area)	Yes, 1-year license issued while Oklahoma tests are completed	Yes	$30 certificate $10 out-of-state license $41 fingerprinting	Yes
Oregon	Early Childhood/ Elementary, Middle/High School Music	3-year Initial 5-year Continuing	PPST or CBT (basic skills), PRAXIS II (content area)	Yes, tests may be waived with experience	Yes	$60 in-state $90 out-of-state $42 fingerprinting	Yes
Pennsylvania	K–12 Music	6-year Instructional I, Permanent Instructional II available after 3 years	PPST (basic skills), PLT (professional), PRAXIS II (content area)	Yes, but all tests are required	Yes, but not in use	$15 certificate	Yes
Rhode Island	K–12 Music	3-year Certificate	PLT (professional)	Yes, Enhanced Reciprocity	No	$25 application	Yes
South Carolina	K–12 Choral, Instrumental, Piano, Violin, Voice	3-year Initial 5-year Professional	PLT (professional), PRAXIS II (content area)	Yes, tests waived with 3 years experience	Yes	$49 application	Yes

159

Certification Practices for Music Educators in the Fifty States							
State	**Certificate Age Levels and Subject Areas**	**Levels and Length of Certification**	**Testing Requirements**	**Reciprocity**	**Alternative Degree Programs**	**Fees**	**Online Forms**
South Dakota	K–12 Vocal, Instrumental, Composite	5-year Certificate	Human Relations and South Dakota Indian Studies courses	Yes, but human relations and Indian courses are required	Yes	$30 certificate $20 out-of-state review	Yes
Tennessee	K–12 Vocal, Instrumental	5-year Apprentice 10-year Professional	PLT (professional), PRAXIS II (content area)	Yes, exemption from testing for experience	Yes	None	Yes
Texas	PreK–12 Music	5-year Standard	ExCET (professional and content area)	Yes, 1-year certificate to complete testing for states without reciprocity	Yes	$75 in-state $175 out-of-state	No
Utah	6–12, K–12 Music	3-year Level I Basic Type, 5-year Level II Standard Type	None	Yes, with equivalent course work	Yes	$15 certificate $15 out-of-state filing	Renewal forms
Vermont	K–6, 7–12, K–12 Music Out-of-state specific areas	2-year Beginning Level I, 7-year Professional Level II	PPST or CBT	Yes, but test is required	Yes	$25 letter of eligibility $35 filing fee $35 per year of license	No
Virginia	PreK–12 Vocal, Instrumental	5-year License	PPST or CBT (basic skills), PRAXIS II (content area)	Yes, testing waived with 2+ years experience	Yes	$50 in-state license $75 out-of-state license $25 renewal fee	Yes
Washington	PreK–12 General, Choral, Instrumental	5-year Residency 5-year Professional	None	Complete application is required	Yes, as intern	$25 certificate $20 initial processing $59 fingerprinting	Yes
West Virginia	PreK–12 Music	3-year Provisional Professional 5-year Professional Permanent	PPST or CBT (basic skills), PLT (professional), PRAXIS II (content area)	Yes, 1-year license to complete testing	No	$15 license $40 fingerprinting	No
Wisconsin	K–6, 7–12, K–12 General 7–12 Choral K–12 Instrumental	5-year Initial 5-year Renewal	PPST or CBT (basic skills), Native American Tribes courses	Accepts other states' basic skills tests, 2 years to complete Native American course	No	$100 in-state license $150 out-of-state license	No
Wyoming	K–6, 5–8, 7–12, K–12 Vocal/General, Instrumental, or Composite	5-year Standard	None, US and Wyoming Constitution course	Yes, but may have renewal requirements	Yes	$125 evaluation $45 fingerprinting	No

Reprinted with permission of the *Journal of Music Teacher Education*

Certification Exam Preparation

As documented in the chart, there are seven states that have no required standardized test for certification. The remaining forty-three states require some combination of tests of basic skills and general knowledge, professional educational knowledge, and music content knowledge. Many states have their own state-developed exams. The PRAXIS series tests developed by the Educational Testing Service in 2001 are required in twenty-one states (the highest number of states requiring the same test). This chapter closes with some detailed information on the PRAXIS Music Tests provided by Debbie Lynn Wolf, one of the chief readers for Educational Testing Services. Many of the state-developed tests are similar in structure and content to the PRAXIS, so all certification students should find this testing discussion useful.

> The PRAXIS Music tests provide an assessment of the knowledge and application of concepts and skills necessary for the beginning music educator. The three current PRAXIS Music tests are described below.
>
> *Music: Content Knowledge (0113)*; multiple choice; 135 questions with 40 based on recorded excerpts; 2 hours; music history and literature, music theory, performance, music learning P–12, professional practices.
>
> *Music: Concepts and Processes (0111)*; constructed response; 2 questions; 1 hour; teaching performance skills (choice of instrumental or choral topics); teaching a musical concept in a general music class.
>
> *Music: Analysis (0112)*; constructed response; 3 questions; 1 hour; error detection of recorded instrumental and choral performances; score analysis for instrumental, choral, or general music teaching
>
> Familiarity with each test, including test content, format, sample questions, testing and scoring procedures, and score requirements is necessary for adequate test preparation. Detailed information on all three music tests, including scoring procedures, sample questions, specific study guidelines, test-taking strategies, and three full-length practice tests, is described in the *Study Guide for the Music Tests: Concepts and Processes; Analysis;* and *Content Knowledge,* a publication of Educational Testing Services. The PRAXIS Web site

(www.ets.org/praxis/index.html) offers an overview, sample questions, and *Tests at a Glance* materials free of charge.

Certification students may be required to take one or more of the three PRAXIS Music tests to qualify for certification. Each state individually determines the type of test and the minimum passing scores. Thus, requirements in nearby states may be different: a score below one state's requirement may be acceptable in a nearby state. Certification students should be aware of the specific PRAXIS requirements for each state in which they are considering teaching in the next few years.

The certification student should realize that studying merely to pass a test is a near-sighted goal. Instead, the certification student should strive to be an excellent music educator, equipped with all the knowledge and skills needed to meet the needs of future students. The knowledge and skills required of a beginning music educator cannot be crammed, but should be accumulated through the entire course of study in the certification program. Actually, professional development, as well as test preparation, begins with the first courses in the program and builds upon the developing musicianship and pedagogical understandings acquired through daily practice and study throughout the certification program. Meeting test score requirements should be a natural result of long-term academic excellence, musical achievement, and professional commitment acquired through course work, extracurricular activities, music study and performance, teaching experiences, and various opportunities related to the music education profession.

While it should not be an end unto itself, preparing for a PRAXIS Music test can have a positive effect on the certification student's development. The benefits of reviewing material to meet state score requirements include sharpening skills and solidifying understandings; thus, test preparation can be viewed as another step in developing the professional music educator. Meeting a score requirement can provide affirmation of possessing the necessary musical background knowledge for the certification student.

Because a PRAXIS Music test is comprehensive, covering information presented in many courses, there is much more material to review than for a final exam. Knowledge from many resources must be integrated and understood as a whole. Adequate preparation and review are necessary to ensure success.

An organized approach to preparing for any comprehensive exam will improve the quality of study and the confidence of the student. The Study Guide provides a comprehensive approach to the review process for the PRAXIS Music tests and outlines a timetable for adequate preparation. For any test, the format and the content specifications of the test should be considered first. Knowing the question format (multiple choice, short answer, essay, constructed response, etc.) to expect and the topics covered on the test narrows the focus. An assessment of the certification student's understanding of each topic covered in the exam should provide a basis for a study plan. Fill in the gaps by reviewing courses and textbooks. Material covered in the PRAXIS Music tests can be found in standard textbooks. Work out a schedule to be sure to cover all the topics specified for each test.

Strategies for test-taking success include getting plenty of rest and nourishment prior to the date of the test, avoiding unnecessary stress by coming prepared and arriving early, wearing comfortable clothes, and bringing a watch. During the test, time must be budgeted. Be aware of the time left to complete the test, and avoid spending too much time on any one question. Answer the known first, then return to the more challenging aspects of the test.

When taking multiple-choice tests such as the Music: Content Knowledge Test, work at a pace that allows for careful reading of each question and all possible answers. A pace that is too fast may cause careless mistakes, confusion, and the need to reread questions. A pace that is too slow may prevent the completion of all the questions. A question should never be left blank because there is no penalty for wrong answers. Stay focused, and remember that no one is supposed to answer every question correctly: don't keep track of mistakes.

When taking constructed response tests such as either Music: Concepts and Processes or Music: Analysis, focus on answering what the question requires with specific details that demonstrate understanding and application of skills. Avoid responses that are too vague or too generalized, or responses that provide superfluous and irrelevant details. Write neatly, but do not concentrate on writing style; focus on the content. A constructed response does not mean an essay: an outline with adequate detailed explanations or sub-points is acceptable. Take time to reread responses to correct ambiguity.

Preparation for a PRAXIS Music test is an opportunity to review and refine your preparation as a music education professional. Develop lifelong habits of study, reflection, and application. Consider the impact you will make on tomorrow's students by investing in your own preparation today and every day.

Chapter Eight
The Job Search

Finding the Job

Every state has different procedures for advertising available jobs. Many state music education associations have a music educators association (MEA) Web site to advertise jobs. The following Web sites may also provide useful information for students looking for jobs as music teachers.

Online Resources for Job Seekers:

MENC–Career Guide: www.menc.org/industry/job/career.html
Music Library Association: www.musiclibraryassoc.org
Monster: www.monster.com
Career Builder: www.careerbuilder.com
Employment Guide: www.employmentguide.com
Information on Music Education:
www.menc.org/information/infoserv/info.htm
Bureau of Labor–Job Outlook: stats.bls.gov/oco/ocos069.htm
Riley Guide: www.rileyguide.com/arts.html
College Board:
www.collegeboard.com/csearch/majors_careers/profiles/majors/100617.html

If you are looking for a job close to campus, you may find that word of mouth is a reliable source. Music education faculty, conductors, applied faculty, and education faculty are often aware of local teaching positions. Most school districts post jobs on school Web sites, so you might begin by targeting school districts in the geographic area you are interested in and keeping a daily watch on their Web sites. Some districts combine resources with other districts and have a hiring organization (which might be called a consortium or a clearinghouse). This means that in order to be hired in a school district the applicant must complete the hiring application put together by the consortium. This often includes an online application and may involve telephone interviews or other types of screening tools.

Job fairs held at your college or university are another good place for finding jobs. Administrators at the job fairs often hold on-site interviews right at the fair. This can be a great place to get a little interviewing experience.

Finding jobs and figuring out what the districts require can take some time, so if you are in job search mode, plan your time accordingly. Most positions will ask for a cover letter, a resume, original transcripts from your college or university, and letters of recommendation. Some schools and communities require the completion of a district application (often online). Others may require a phone interview or personality test to be done online. More details regarding these are in the next section.

Cover Letters

We suggest sending a specific cover letter to each job you are applying for rather than a generic cover letter that goes to all. Use the name of the school district and some of the details of the job description in the cover letter. Each cover letter that you write may be slightly different to accommodate for the needs of the job.

Resumes

Most jobs will ask for a resume. Some may use the term vitae, which is short for curriculum vitae. A resume is usually shorter (some say keep to one page) and a vitae is more extensive. Unless it is specified that the resume be only one page, we suggest a two- to three-page resume.

We recommend that resumes be created on plain white paper without fancy graphics using 12-point font. There are numerous templates available for resume creation. Many of these begin with an objective. In music education, the objective is to seek a position as a music teacher, so it is unnecessary to include this on a music education resume. Some templates also provide a space for a statement of philosophy. Unless the job asks for this information specifically, once again we suggest using the limited resume space for information regarding your background and experience rather than your philosophy. There will be time to discuss philosophy in an interview or on the job application.

Be extremely accurate on all the documents you submit. There can be no typographical errors. Have multiple people read your materials carefully before you send them out. Proofread, proofread, and then proofread again. Sections of the resume may include (in this order):

- Contact Information
- Education and Certification
- Teaching Experience
- Intern Experience
- Performance Experience
- Other Work Experience
- Honors and Awards
- Professional Organizations
- Other Interests
- References

Depending on your background and experience, some sections may need to be cut in order to keep the resume under three pages.

Contact information. Be sure to list all contact information (name, address, telephone, and e-mail) clearly at the top of the resume. If you are moving from a dorm or an apartment over the summer you might list a current address and a permanent address (possibly your parents'). If you are relocating to a new town and state and can list a local address near the school, this can be helpful. Be sure that the e-mail listed is one that you have access to. If you have an odd e-mail name (e.g., sexycellist@wherever.edu) you should consider a new account with a more professional name. The same idea is true for your answering machine or cell phone message. Be sure the first contact that a potential employer makes with you is professional. You may need to alert roommates or housemates that potential employers may call.

Education and certification. List all degrees earned starting with the most recent degree. Write out the name of the degree (e.g., bachelor of music instead of BM). You might include your grade point average if it is impressive. If you are in a state that has P–12 music certification, we suggest calling your degree "music education" and not "choral music education" or "instrumental music education." There will be opportunities later on the resume to highlight your specialization. In fact, you might want to format the resume in slightly different ways for different jobs. If you are applying for an elementary job in one community and a secondary job in another you may tweak the document to highlight the needs of the job you are applying for. List your high school graduation as well. Finally, include information regarding certification.

Teaching Experience. If you have teaching experience beyond student teaching, list that in a separate section called Teaching Experience and then list student teaching and other intern work in a separate section called Intern Experience. The teaching experience section should include any teaching you were paid to do. This might include marching band camps or instrumental or vocal sectional work, private lessons, or music camp counseling. Keep this section to only music teaching experiences. Other types of experiences can be placed in Other Work Experience.

List the teaching by date in backwards order (most recent experience first). Include a few points about your responsibilities on that job and list a contact person, if possible. Do not include teaching you may have done while you were still a student in high school. If you have very little teaching experience other than student teaching, you may have just one section called "teaching experience," which includes your work as an intern.

Intern experience. Student teaching and any other intern experience (preservice fieldwork) should be listed in this section. The format should be the same as in the section above. Include a few points about your responsibilities, and list a contact person. Be sure to include dates of the experience (some may be short time frames for preservice fieldwork). Do not include observation fieldwork, just situations in which you had the opportunity to teach.

Performance experience. List any professional performance experiences you may have in addition to campus ensemble experiences. Do not list performances from high school. Keep this section short. You want the employer to know that you are a musician, but you do not want them to think that you are more interested in performance than in teaching. Include the date(s) of the performance experience.

Other work experience. This is the section where you may list other jobs (non-music) that you have held. Keep this section short, and just list a few of your work experiences. As always, list them in backwards order by date, and include some of the duties and a contact person. It is important for potential employers to know that you have had the experience of showing up to work and doing a job even if that job was outside of music teaching. If you list solid teaching experience earlier in the document, you may consider cutting this section.

Honors and awards. If you received any honors or awards as a student, list those here. Do not include awards from high school. If you do not have any awards, just leave this section out.

Professional organizations. List your membership in professional music organizations (e.g., MENC, ACDA, ASTA). Write out the name of the organization, and include any office you may have held in a local chapter of these groups. If you are not a member of any professional organization, join one immediately so that you can include this information. We cannot overemphasize the importance of joining one or more professional music teacher organizations and remaining an active member throughout your teaching career.

Other interests. If you have other interests you think would be desirable to a school (e.g., experience in coaching or drama), list those interests here. This section is not an absolute necessity.

References. We suggest listing four or five professional references right on the resume. Some resume templates suggest using the phrase "references are available upon request." However, we think that potential employers are happy to have this information supplied. Be sure to contact everyone whom you intend to list as a reference before posting them on your resume. List the name of the person and their title (in relationship to you). For example: "John Smith, Middle School Band Director and Co-operating Teacher for Middle School Student Teaching Placement." Include the person's address, telephone, and e-mail. Do not list more than four or five references even if twenty people are willing to be references for you. The employer does not want to have to choose from a long list. Some of these references may be the same contacts listed elsewhere on your resume.

You might change the list of references depending on the job. If the job is middle school choral, you might include a campus faculty member in choral music, whereas for an elementary general music position you might include a campus elementary general music faculty member instead. Try to choose references who can speak to your work with children in a school setting and not just to your work on campus.

Transcripts

Many employers will ask for official transcripts from your college or university. These are usually ordered through the college or university registrar's office and may take several weeks to process. There is usually a fee for sending transcripts. Be sure to leave time for the process as you consider application deadlines. Purchase an unofficial transcript for yourself so you can bring it to an interview in the event that your official ones have not arrived. Many institutions have a campus placement office or credential file center. These centers will often send your resume, transcripts, and recommendation letters out to any employer upon your request. Contact the student services office at your school to see if there is such an office and to get details about setting up a placement file.

Letters of Recommendation

Most jobs require three letters of recommendation. They will often stipulate that the letters be confidential. This means that the person who writes the letter sends it directly to the placement office or the school and knows that the prospective teacher did not see the letter. Ask someone to write you a confidential letter only if you are sure that the person writing the letter will be completely supportive of you and your work. If you are not sure, do not ask for a confidential letter.

It is fine for the references on your resume to be the same people who write your letters of recommendation. Be sure to give the recommendation letter writers time to write the letter. We suggest several weeks. Provide them with a copy of your resume so the letter writer can be reminded of your background and accomplishments. In most cases, you will leave a letter cover sheet for the person. The person will complete the cover sheet and the letter and then send the letter directly to the placement office or the school. You should provide the letter writer with a stamped envelope so that there is no cost to the letter writer. Many placement offices are now doing recommendation letters in an online format. Either way, be sure to give the person time to write and be sure to follow up with a thank you letter.

School District Applications

Many school districts have job applications that must be completed online. Questions on these applications usually mirror information you have already gathered for your resume, curriculum vitae, or portfolio. Some of these applications include essays or short answer questions that are more like the interview questions at the end of this chapter (classroom management, planning, assessment, etc.). Take care to respond carefully to the application as the search committee may screen applicants based on the online application before they ever consider hard copy materials.

Communication with the Schools

Most schools will not begin calling candidates for interviews until after the application deadline for the position. It is fine to contact the school to be sure that all your materials have arrived. However, we would suggest that you do not contact the school more than once before the application deadline. After the deadline, schools will begin to contact candidates for interviews. They will often interview several rounds of candidates before letting applicants know that the position has been filled. What this may mean is that weeks (maybe even months) will go by while you do not hear anything from some of the places where you have applied.

It is appropriate to contact the school to inquire about where they are in their search. If they have begun interviews, they may let you know that. Or they may not. As frustrating as it may be, a lot of waiting takes place at this point in the process. Continue to put applications in to many schools even if you think that you will get one of the positions you have applied for. Keep all of your options open until you sign a contract.

Interviewing for a Job as a Music Teacher

First impressions are very important at a job interview. Arrive early so you have time to prepare before walking into the interview. Dress professionally. We suggest a suit for both men and women. Men should wear a tie. Even if you do not intend to dress conservatively for school every day, dress conservatively for the interview. Bring copies of your transcripts and resume as well as your teaching portfolio (the one described in Chapter Four). Leave your cell phone in the car! If possible, gather details about the music program at the school and information about the community from the Web. Then try to incorporate what you have learned about the school and the music program in your interactions during the interview.

Most interviews center on core questions, so it is possible to prepare for the interview by practicing your answers to typical questions in advance. We suggest writing out responses to common interview questions and then practice articulating the response. In addition to practicing your interview answers, practice confident interview posture (standing and seated), hand gestures, your handshake, a confident smile, and eye contact. Videotape a mock interview, and watch for your level of confidence and engagement. Most members of search committees for P–12 music positions come to the committee thinking "Is this someone I would want my own child to spend time with in a classroom?" Show your passion for students and teaching in every interview response. The more experience you have, even in a mock interview setting, the more successful you will be at the real interview.

Sample Job Interview Topics and Questions

General Topics and Questions
- Tell us about yourself.
- Tell us about your strengths and weaknesses.
- Why did you decide to become a teacher?
- In what ways would you be an asset to our school?
- Where do you see yourself in five to ten years?
- Do you have any questions for us?

Classroom Management

- What kinds of management issues do you think could potentially occur in your classroom, and how would you deal with them?
- Discuss your expectations for behavior and what the consequences will be for misbehavior.
- How will you manage your ensemble when you are working with one section at a time?
- Describe a classroom management problem and how you would deal with it.
- Do you expect to handle most management issues yourself, or will you seek help from administrators from time to time? Cite a few examples.

Planning for Instruction/Rehearsal Techniques

- Describe a typical daily rehearsal or music class.
- How will you account for varying achievement levels in your classroom?
- What teaching strategies are you going to use to make your rehearsal/music class more effective?
- What will your warm-up/start-of-class procedure look like?

Designing Curriculum

- Do you have any experience in designing curricula?
- What teaching philosophies would you like to see incorporated into the curriculum?
- Why should music be a part of the school curriculum? Isn't it more suitable for an extracurricular activity?
- Will you bring music theory and history into your performing class? If so, how?
- How do you intend to integrate other content areas into your classroom?
- How will you create a standards-based curriculum?
- How would you define a comprehensive musician?
- How do you see the music program fitting in with the context of the rest of the school?

Choosing Literature and Concert Planning (for Ensembles)

- What goals are involved in concert performance? Why do you have concerts?

- How will you deal with a student who has a scheduling conflict with a concert?
- Describe a few pieces suitable for _____ grade band (orchestra or choir) that you like and why.
- What resources do you know of that will help you choose appropriate literature?
- What are some characteristics of "good" literature for this age group?
- Discuss issues associated with choosing literature and concert programming. What do you expect will be the balance between performing and other activities in your music classroom?
- How will you go about educating your audience with regard to literature?

Student Assessment

- How will you grade the students in your class?
- How do you plan to assess your music students?
- Will you make use of singing/playing (performance) and/or written tests? How will you grade these fairly?
- What sorts of skills/knowledge will you assess? How?
- What is the goal for your students as they leave the classroom? How will you assess whether they have reached that goal?
- Discuss some of the ways you will assess your impact as a teacher.

Competitions and Festivals (for Ensembles)

- Is participation in a competition/festival part of your educational plan?
- How would you react to a bad rating? How would you talk about it with your ensemble?
- What are your views on a chair/seating system?
- Is competition within ensembles important?
- How would you praise your accomplished performers without making your less talented performers feel bad?

Administrative Duties of the Secondary Teacher

- How will you stay organized when interacting with students, teachers, parents, and others?
- How will you oversee additional financial endeavors such as fund-raising?
- What types of fund-raising do you find beneficial and successful?
- How will you communicate daily/weekly/semester expectations to your students?

Program Advocacy

- Why is your music program a valuable activity?
- Why are music programs different and more unique than other activities/sports?
- In what sort of community events do you plan to participate?
- What is your plan for parental and community involvement and cooperation?

Working with Children of Special Needs

- Do you have any experience working with children of special needs?
- How will you incorporate special needs students in your classroom?
- Do you support the inclusion model of instruction?
- Would you be comfortable participating in or do you have experience with the IEP (Individual Education Plan) process?

Pedagogy

Be prepared to describe your sequence for teaching some area of content specific to the job. For example, in a string interview you may be asked to describe the teaching of shifting. In a band interview you may be asked to teach a clarinet embouchure. The possibilities are endless. Think about how to articulate your pedagogical beliefs.

Professional Development

- What will you do to stay active in the field?
- What professional development plans do you have?

We suggest practicing responses to these various questions with peers or mentors. Try to include specific musical examples for questions about music, and try to include specific instructional examples you have used in your responses regarding education. It is okay to say that you don't know or have no experience with something you are unfamiliar with. Be confident, but don't try to pretend that you know it all. When a district hires a beginning teacher they are looking for potential, and they realize you have a lot to learn. They like to see that you know you have a lot to learn as well.

Second- and Third-Round Interviews

In some situations there will be multiple interviews for the position. The first interview may be a phone screen interview, or it may be an in-person interview primarily for the purpose of reducing the size of the candidate pool. If you get called for a second interview, there was something they liked about you; otherwise they would not call you back. Sometimes the music teachers or a building principal do the first-round interviews, and upper-level district administrators get involved in the second or third round. The second or third round often includes a teaching demonstration. If the committee chair does not present information regarding salary and benefits, it is appropriate to ask about these details in the final interview.

Music Teaching at the Interview

For some positions you may be asked to teach a sample lesson as part of the interview process. You may conduct a rehearsal or work with a group of general music students. In some cases you may receive scores or materials in advance, and in other settings you may just be put in front of a group of students for a period of time (usually twenty minutes or so). The goal of this type of activity is to get a sense of your rapport and interaction with students and to get a glimpse of your musicianship. Work to show both qualities in your teaching presentation. If possible, find a way to model musically either with your instrument or voice. Engage students, and try to get to know them in the time that you are given. Your interaction with the students is more important than the content of your lesson.

Teaching in Low-Income Schools and the Repayment of Loans

There are several programs that offer loan cancellation and other financial benefits to teachers in rural and/or low-income schools. The following Web sites contain more information about specific loans and repayment criteria:

Poverty Standards: www.census.gov/hhes/poverty/povdef.html
Perkins Loan: studentaid.ed.gov/
Perkins Loan: baowww.uoregon.edu/Student/Perkins.htm
Stafford Loan: www.salliemae.com/apply/borrowing/stafford.html
Stafford Loan: studentaid.ed.gov
Loan Forgiveness: www.aft.org/teachers/jft/loanforgiveness.htm
State Incentive Policies: www.ecs.org/clearinghouse/39/16/3916.htm
Small School Achievement Program:
www.ed.gov/programs/reapsrsa/eligibility.html?src=mr

Research Base for Student Teaching in Music

Brand, M. 1982. Effects of student teaching on the classroom management beliefs and skills of music teachers. *Journal of Research in Music Education* 30(4), 255–265.

Broyles, J. 1997. Effects of videotape analysis on role development of student teachers in music. PhD diss., University of Oklahoma, 1997.

Feiman, S., and M. Buchmann. 1987. When is student teaching teacher education? *Teaching and Teacher Education* 3, 255–273.

Rideout, R., and A. Feldman. 2001. Research in music student teaching. In *The new handbook of music teaching and learning*, ed. R. Colwell and C. P. Richardson, 874–886. New York: Oxford.

Suggested Readings for Student Teaching in Music

Campbell, M. R. 2002. Professional teaching portfolios: For pros and preservice teachers alike. *Music Educators Journal* 89(2): 25–31.

Kersten, F. 2004. E-portfolios for the Internet job hunt. *Teaching Music* 11(4): 40–47.

Music Educators National Conference. 2004. Need help finding your first job? In *Spotlight on transition to teaching music*. Reston, VA: MENC.

———. 2004. What's so hard about student teaching? In *Spotlight on transition to teaching music*. Reston, VA: MENC.

Pelletier, C. M. 2004. *Strategies for successful student teaching: A comprehensive guide*. 2nd ed. Boston: Pearson.

Podsen, I., and V. M. Denmark. 2000. *Coaching and mentoring first-year and student teachers*. Larchmont, NY: Eye on Education.

Roe, B. D., and E. P. Ross. 2002. *Student teaching and field experiences handbook*. 5th ed. Upper Saddle River, NJ: Prentice-Hall.

Part Three:

The First Years as a Music Teacher

Chapter Nine
Challenges Faced by
Beginning Music Teachers

There is considerable research on the challenges faced by beginning music teachers (see Suggested Reading). Rather than creating a long list of tips for the first-year teacher to attend to, the following two chapters provide first-person narrative accounts of beginning music teachers' experiences. Each story concludes with some questions for novice teachers to consider. The real life stories depicted here are not intended to scare but to get you thinking about strategies for the early years of teaching.

The first two stories are classic descriptions of classroom management struggles. Classroom management is the single most well documented challenge for all beginning teachers, including music teachers. Dan and Armand both provide some excellent classroom management strategies mixed in with their personal reflections.

I Shudder to Remember!

I had a huge learning curve for classroom management my first year of teaching. My rehearsals were erratic because I could not consistently manage my students' behavior. Student teaching never really prepared me for classroom management because I worked with an experienced co-operating teacher. Some experiences from my first year of teaching now make me shudder.

I will always remember the rehearsal I had with my seventh and eighth grade concert band during the last period before holiday vacation. I saw this day coming for weeks and brainstormed strategies with my mentor as to what to do. My mentor advised against doing any real work like sight-reading or rehearsing. She said the hassle of getting students to do work on the Friday before vacation was just not worth the misery. A party was out of the question. Many students already had too much sugar in them. She advised doing something fun to keep them active and interested.

I came up with the idea of playing some easy arrangements of holiday songs to engage them. I gathered all the parts, put them on their chairs, made percussion assignments, set up the stage, typed up a lesson plan, the whole nine yards. I thought, "If this bombs, you can't fault me for not being prepared!"

After hours of anticipation, the last period arrived. The students came in complaining. "Aww, do we have to play, Mr. Albert?" In my stern manner, I said, "Yes, good bands practice at their highest level every day." They all brought their instruments; they knew me well enough by that time to know that they were going to play regardless.

The students sat and listened to my instructions. We got the first piece out and played through. It was all right, but, being me, I had to correct some musical issues. I got closer to a section I wanted to help. As I started to work with them, students on the opposite side of the stage played completely random stuff. Out of the corner of my eye, I saw students run out of their seats and around the stage area before spilling into the audience section while playing their instruments.

"Oh no, here we go...right when things were going so well!" I thought. I had to stop what I was doing and get those students in their seats before I lost control of the class. While I was doing that, the students I was working with played random wild and extremely loud notes that completely overpowered my voice. Within two minutes, the class had descended into total chaos. The percussionists were banging on the drums, some students were loudly playing onstage, and others were in the audience section running around like it was the gymnasium. I totally lost control of the class and felt completely helpless. I thought that if my principal walked in and saw this I was going to be fired on the spot.

I yelled and yelled until my voice was hoarse. I made it known that I was furious, hoping it would help convince the deviant students to get back onstage and behave. I got most of the students back up onstage in some semblance of order, but the atmosphere was just too unsettled. The students knew that the rehearsal was just a big joke, and that's the way it was for thirty-five minutes—a big joke. I worked with some students on the music in vain while monitoring crowd control by making sure students stayed onstage and in sight.

The bell rang signaling the end of my misery. After all my students left, I sat on stage for ten minutes, my body wrapped up in a ball. I was totally shocked and depressed. Then I tried looking at the bright side. "Well, things can only look up from here."

They did. Overall, it was a successful year. After a few years of experience, classroom management is gradually getting easier for me. Learning experiences like the one I just described helped me to realize what I needed to do to maintain a classroom environment conductive to learning. I still have bad days, but I just need to think about what I could have done better and say to myself: "Things can only look up from here."

—Dan Albert

Questions for Discussion

• Taking into account the time the band rehearsal was going to take place, what could you have planned to do for the rehearsal?

• What actions do you think Dan could have taken when he realized the rehearsal was starting to spiral out of control?

• What could Dan have done during and after the chaos to bring the rehearsal back to a controlled state?

• If Dan wanted to teach the same plan, what could he have done at the beginning of class, if anything, to prevent this from happening?

• Taking into account that all the students were misbehaving, would you punish all the students, a select few, or none? Why or why not? What punishment do you think would be appropriate?

• Is there anything the band students could learn from this experience? If so, what? How would you try to facilitate learning?

• What were some proactive actions Dan took to try to make this rehearsal successful? Is there anything else he could have done?

• Why did Dan's plan ultimately fail?

Classroom Management Tips I Now Know

Over the past three years I have finally realized classroom management is not about controlling the students. The control of the students is just a byproduct of thorough planning by the teacher. In my first year, I made a big mistake by only placing the class rules in the band handbook. I thought that doing this and having the students and parents sign a form stating they had read the rules would be enough for me to get successful results. I knew that if it ever came down to an argument with the parents I could use the signed form as leverage to win the argument. I have done this a few times, but I really did not gain the results I wanted. I am now more interested in having the class run smoothly, allowing me to do my job—teach music.

I still use the list of rules in the band handbook but I think the addition of visual aids in the classroom next year will allow me to focus on the students more. I remember the look of utter confusion upon one student's face when I referenced a rule in the handbook stating that students who play the piano without approval will receive a detention. He didn't remember the rules he had read in the handbook in September only three months later. We both could have saved time and frustration if I had taken the extra step of placing a sign with the rule over the pianos.

I have four dry erase boards in my classroom where I put up what each band will play each day. Once the students learn to use the boards in their set-up it is very useful. I have noticed more behavior problems on days in which I did not write the music schedule on the boards. The same thing happens if I do not follow the flow of the board. I need to continue to go that extra mile to make sure that the boards are always accurate.

When my students begin the sixth grade I have them line up outside along the wall in front of the band room. This calms them down and focuses their attention on playing their instruments. I have noticed that on days I don't remind them to not talk, they enter the classroom more rambunctiously. I spend more time getting them settled in the classroom than it would have taken for me to quiet them down in the hallway. I try to play a piece of music for them every day when the class starts. This way they are focusing on the right things. However, the class begins hectically if I do not play a piece of music or allow some of the students to talk without penalty.

We all try to find ways to keep the other students busy and quiet while we work with one section. I used to ask for the students to listen to the group I was working with and allowed them to comment on the group's playing. This idea went very well for a while. When I moved on with the class, however, the students did not feel involved in the process anymore, and I began to battle talking during sectional work. I know another teacher who places a sheet in students' folders to remind them how to behave during sectional work time, which is an easy step that will help in the long run.

I was very concerned about concert etiquette when going out in public. I used to admonish students to act appropriately before taking them out to concerts. Later, I found it easier and more effective to practice concert etiquette as a part of our everyday process. I taught the students how to clap appropriately, and I banished any laughing or negative commentary while others were playing. The students began to accept these actions as the norm and displayed them in public rather easily.

All of the classroom management problems I have listed could have been accomplished by the simple tasks of placing a sign up above the piano or always having a piece of music to play for the students. It was my lack of organizational foresight that caused the students to lose focus. Classroom management is not a secret or a set of perfect rules and directions. It is a constantly evolving situation with the teacher trying to focus the students on a well designed, planned, and consistent classroom.

—Armand Hall

Questions for Discussion

- What is most important to me in my rehearsal?
- What type of room do I want? (Strict, relaxed, fun, serious?)
- What do I find myself repeating the most during class?
- Is a band handbook worth making? What rules in the handbook do I have the most trouble with?
- What can I set in place now (e.g., concert etiquette) that will produce the results I want in the future?
- What visual aids can I create to reiterate the rules?

Teaching in areas where you feel ill prepared is one of the most common concerns of all beginning music teachers. For music educators (who earn a P–12 certification in most states) this challenge can be even more daunting. Corynn's story describes her growth from being fearful of non-band classrooms to deciding she might just like to stay "outside."

Teaching Outside of My Comfort Area

When I first graduated and began seeking employment as a music teacher, preferably in a beginning and middle school band position, I encountered a number of unexpected obstacles. Some of these obstacles were beyond my control. The job market was not very open because many programs were consolidating. Instead of hiring a new teacher to replace one just retired, current teachers were simply asked to take on more responsibilities. Another roadblock was that where I live it is difficult to find available teaching jobs posted. I had to rely on word of mouth and intensive online searches, going to the human resources page of every nearby district.

However, I created other problems for myself. Having married just after graduating, my husband and I decided that we would move wherever the first person to get a job was hired: he won. This limited my choices. More of a problem, though, was my hesitancy to apply for music jobs outside of my specific content area. This left me with fewer opportunities.

Needless to say, the only job offers I received were much too far away to accept, so the school year began, and I remained unemployed. I applied as a substitute teacher in the local school district with little pleasure as I considered a year of subbing here and there in all different kinds of classrooms. I also contacted the fine arts director and mentioned that I was available if any long-term music substitute teacher was needed. This proved to be the best move I made in my entire job search: in doing so, I have been employed almost the entire school year in different long-term music positions. The catch: not one of these positions has been in my content area.

This "catch" turned out to be the most educational experience I've had as a music teacher. My first position involved teaching elementary strings and percussion. Though I would have

---

184

gladly accepted a job teaching beginning percussion, the idea of teaching beginning string orchestras almost made me decline the position because I doubted myself so much. By taking that job, I now know that it is not only possible to stay one step ahead of the students in order to teach each lesson—it can also be fun! As a result, I am more confident in my abilities as a music teacher and am a much better string player.

My second position was in an elementary general music classroom. Once again, I almost decided to decline the position. Whereas I had a full year of string methods to carry me through the two months of teaching beginning strings, I had not one bit of experience in elementary general music. This position proved to be even more educational, as the teacher for whom I was subbing guided me through lesson plans and helped me come up with creative ways to teach the curriculum. I left that position with a confidence I would never have known just by study and observation in a class.

My current position is in another elementary general classroom until the end of the school year. The district provided me with a mentor, but I am solely responsible for teaching the curriculum and assessment, and for preparing a fourth and fifth grade program. I am thankful that I had the courage to look beyond my doubts and venture into other content areas; how could I possibly have known that I would enjoy elementary general music as much or more than beginning band or orchestra?

Besides location, being so strongly tied to my content area proved to be the most limiting effect on my efforts to find a job. Teaching outside of my content area has not only given me insight into and knowledge of other areas, it has provided the opportunity to look at my own content area through different eyes. My perception of myself as a music teacher has changed enormously, and I believe that my concept of instrumental music education—namely, band—has widened. In my job search for next year, I'll be much more apt to apply for positions that don't quite fit my niche.

—Corynn Nordstrom

Questions for Discussion

- As music teachers with specific content areas, what are our fears about teaching outside of our comfort zones?
- Why do these fears keep us from considering teaching outside our content areas?
- Do you believe it is possible to successfully teach one step ahead of your students? Why or why not?
- Teaching outside of your content area can be challenging and require extra learning and practice on your part. Would this deter you from applying for or accepting a teaching job outside of your content area?
- What do you think could be gained by teaching outside of your content area?

Beginning teachers are rarely prepared for dealing with student tragedy, yet many teachers must deal with such issues. Rebecca's story highlights challenges associated with student illness.

Over the Break

"Ms. Biber...I think something's wrong with Annie." The polite but insistent way they got my attention was typical of students in my seventh grade band. We had a real bond: I would make jokes from the podium, and in return they would give me their attention when I was serious, even if it meant tuning a section three times when half the class was still straining to hear sharp and flat. We were in the middle of rehearsal when I put down the baton and looked at Annie, the second clarinetist in the second row. She had her hands up to her face and looked as though she was sobbing, shaking quietly in her seat. I went over to her, and the class fell silent.

"Annie? What's wrong?" I think I asked. "Annie, can you hear me?" The rest happened fast, in that cool, streamlined space of crisis when thought and action coincide. I remember picking up the classroom phone and dialing the office, asking for a nurse to be sent to the band room. "We have a student who appears to be having a seizure." There was no nurse in the building, but the secretary called an ambulance and in the meantime sent down the assistant principal.

It seemed she took forever to get there. I shouted loudly in that full, silent room, "Annie, you're going to be fine. Try to stay awake." I held up her head, which kept lolling back, with my left hand. Once the assistant principal arrived, someone else was in charge. She dismissed the class, and the students put away their instruments quietly and left. She got Annie on her feet with my help, and we tried to walk her around. She moved in and out of consciousness.

It was not long before the paramedics arrived. They got Annie to open her eyes. On the stretcher she told the medics that she had taken some pills. She didn't know how many, and she didn't know what kind. Someone sent for Annie's sister, a year older. She cried to see Annie on the stretcher and rode with her in the ambulance.

While Annie went to the hospital I attempted to teach the rest of my daily classes. In the following days, her band mates made huge cards out of colorful paper and markers. A few boys took up a collection of quarters and dollars for a bouquet. I don't think they felt sorry for Annie, but they did love her, as I did too. She was beautiful, outgoing, and an average musician, but she was especially well liked by students and teachers. Her older sister was quiet, and more reserved, but we learned in the coming months that both suffered from some form of depression that caused them either to fall ill or to try to harm themselves.

Once she had partially recovered, Annie sent her classmates and me a thank you card with some stickers and a message that she had "cried happy tears" when she received our tributes. I shared it with the class and still have it among my letters. It was a long time before Annie returned to school.

In teaching, I'd felt I had a sensitivity that helped me connect with certain students. It was the public face of the depression I struggled with. I thought about what to say to Annie as she fell prey to mental illness. So I wrote her a long letter about how I lived with many of the same feelings she did. "You don't have to keep it private," I wrote to her. "You can talk to people who care about you."

It has been two years since I saw my student for who she really was and showed myself to her in return. I could not have empathized so well had I not experienced depression; in this way I found a use for my own disorder. In retrospect, though, I question whether it was proper or professional to share my personal issues with a student, and I wonder whether I would do it again.   —Rebecca Biber

Questions for Discussion

- What kinds of privacy issues are at stake when a student endangers his or her own life? Is there a right to keep the matter in the family?
- How should new teachers be prepared to deal with mental illness? Are they currently prepared in any way by their degree-granting institutions?
- How would you have handled this situation if you were the teacher?

Chapter Ten
Continuing Challenges
Faced by Music Teachers

This chapter includes stories from teachers in their second, third, and fourth years of teaching. These stories reflect some concerns that challenge music teachers throughout their careers. This first story focuses on the lack of curricular materials provided to music teachers. Research suggests that focusing on issues of teaching and learning (and long-term curricular goals) are rarely addressed in the first year, and it is not until the second or third year that beginning music teachers start to worry about the curriculum. Stephanie Perry is starting to worry.

In Search of the Curriculum

Sometime during my second year of teaching, the obvious hit me: if I had been teaching another subject, I wouldn't be creating nearly as much material for my classes. Staring at my computer screen, I realized with temporary envy that many other teachers had full books of assignment worksheets, problem sets, and lab procedures in their subject areas. After all, when was the last time I saw a science teacher running down the hall, goggles askew, apologizing for setting off the fire alarm while trying to design an experiment for a chemistry class? Or found the last car in the parking lot to be the English teacher's, who was staying late to complete the final chapter of a book for Freshman Literature? Yet there I was, creating yet another weekly practice assignment from scratch with no more guidance than the research I'd done over the summer and the previous assignments I'd designed when I knew even less. Since I began teaching, I have made up assignments, selected all quiz material, created emergency substitute worksheets, chosen each concert program, designed rubrics for approximately twenty-five different projects, and even written music for my class when my library failed me. I consider myself to be an independent person, but wasn't all this taking self-reliance a little far?

To tell a newly graduated physics major to "teach science" would be laughably inadequate instructions for planning the entire school year. How would the new teacher know what the students had already learned, what they were expected to learn that year, and what knowledge they needed to be successful in subsequent classes? This information is critical for all teachers, not just teachers of the acknowledged academic subjects, yet "teach music" is often the only instruction beginning band directors are given. It seems that this is too large an omission to be ignored, but at the start of my first year of teaching, I hardly noticed. Teaching music was all I had time to think about. So many other concerns claimed my attention first that curricular questions went unasked and unanswered.

Much like the myth of the Loch Ness monster, there is said to exist a district-wide P–12 music curriculum. Disbelief in its existence is common, yet it surfaces occasionally in nearly mythical references. There were even credible rumors in the fall that this was the year music teachers would be charged with revising it, and I thought for a fleeting moment I might catch a glimpse of what I'm supposed to be teaching on paper. But like many good ideas, this one was jettisoned for lack of funding. Even if I had been presented with a binder full of benchmarks and standards when I entered the district, it is unlikely that I would have used them. More probably, I would have glanced at the middle school section and found a place for it on my shelf with other reference material I rarely consult. I don't believe I would have realized the importance of a defined curriculum at that time. When individual days on end were a struggle, planning beyond a week was nearly impossible, and a full year was something that could not be fathomed. My inability to see anything beyond the immediate present prevented me from accurately determining what my students already knew and from predicting how long it would take them to learn new concepts.

I remember staring blankly at scores a week before school began, wondering what would be too hard or too easy, with my own experience on trombone as my inadequate guide. I had no idea what middle school students at each grade level should or could play and learned mainly by trial and error. A curricular framework would have given me a better idea about students' general knowledge and capabilities, assuming that the instruction had been consistently implemented before my arrival, and would also have helped me project their learning over the course of a school year. This year, as I see the results of previously taught concepts raising my students' performance achievements, I've realized the importance of a long-term plan. As I am no longer routinely overwhelmed by the daily demands of teaching, I have started to think several years into the future. The possibilities are exciting–how much better would my bands be if I had an articulated plan for student learning through the middle school years? How much further could we go?

The curriculum I envision is one that guides, not limits, my teaching. I don't envy the social studies teacher who has four civics classes per day and teaches the same concepts the same way each year. Nor do I want a curriculum imposed on me that constrains the freedom I have as a music educator to teach creatively. While I believe curricular goals, once determined, should be assessed, I also fear that too much emphasis on assessment will lead to too strong a focus on isolated skills instead of music as a whole.

These concerns will remain unanswered until the new music curriculum is put into place. While as a second-year teacher I still have much to learn about being a music educator, I look forward to contributing to the revision as best my experience allows. I know that a defined curricular framework will improve my teaching by guiding my long-term planning and will also make more apparent to others outside the profession the depth of what we do when we "teach music."

–Stephanie E. Perry

Questions for Discussion

• What does "teach music" mean to you? How is this the same or different from a typical curricular framework?
• What are the consequences (both positive and negative) for the use or non-use of a curricular framework for a music department?
• Do you think that beginning teachers can effectively implement a curriculum independently? If not, what resources might help them? How might a first-year teacher benefit from a district curriculum?
• Why do you think formal curricula are sometimes ignored by teachers? What changes might make them more useful to a

practicing teacher? What changes might a teacher make in practice to increase a curriculum's utility?

• Discuss curricular assessment.

This next story describes the experiences of a music teacher who taught in one community for three years and then returned to teaching after a year of graduate school in a very different community and teaching context. Many states define a beginning teacher as one who is new to the school, and Andy's story supports this definition.

First-Year Teacher—Again

I taught for three years in a traditional instrumental band program in a small school district neighboring a medium-sized Midwestern city. As the only instrumental music teacher for grades five through twelve, I managed to revitalize the program through improving the dedication, musicianship, and performances of the students involved. I called on the experiences I had as a student in an instrumental music program, learned tricks of the trade through wise and poor judgment on the job, and envisioned myself in a similar role throughout my career. However, opportunities knocked and plans changed.

After a year in graduate school, I jumped at the chance to live and work in New York City at a prep school. The duties included general music for seventh and eighth grade students and assisting all other instrumental and vocal ensembles in any way possible. They wanted me because of the skills and experience I offered, and I took the job because of the unique excitement it offered.

There were huge contrasts to my previous job. I taught only seventh and eighth grade, two of the most notoriously challenging grades to teach in any school. General music was the focus rather than instrumental music. I was in a department of four instead of flying solo. The class sizes were much smaller, and the facilities and resources available were top notch. I was in a small classroom and not a large band room. I would not be giving grades to the students. The socioeconomic make-up of the student body was mostly upper class.

I went into the job without a great deal of preparation. I spent the summer selling off two cars and a house, finding a place to live in New York City, and conducting research for and writing a thesis. I asked my coworkers for ideas of what had been done before, but they admitted to teaching to their strengths when they were in my position and suggested I do the same. I proceeded with a curriculum I was familiar with and felt confident implementing.

Naturally, I had trouble. There were just too many new things to learn. I was experiencing class control issues and was not feeling very confident in my abilities in my new position. Fortunately, I had been a beginning teacher before and knew that the first semester is always a drag. The magic ingredient that is missing for any new teacher is rapport. Based on the fact that the teacher I replaced was let go because of his inability to adequately teach or control the class, I was afraid I would not get the chance to gain any rapport.

It did not help that my administrators did not provide any kind of constructive evaluation of my performance as an educator. Within my department, I was somewhat isolated in that the other three individuals had worked together for several years and shared an office while my room did not adjoin that office. There was never an official departmental meeting, and there was poor interdepartmental communication. I was forced to learn some things about the music program's operations and procedures by making mistakes and having them corrected or rectified. As a result, I began to perceive myself as somewhat of an outsider within the department.

The first meetings with the school's director were often uncomfortable. Apparently, I was causing some concern among my students' parents as the students adjusted to my personality and style. The director was patient, but her responsibility to keep the parents happy was evident, and the contents of the meetings were concerned with addressing all of the negative points and ramifications of my performance.

The crowning moment of my feelings of isolation and inadequacy came after the first concert. I worked hard with the students to have them perform using many classroom instruments, such as percussion and guitars. It was something new and different for the program, and my colleagues and director had hired me partly because of the change I could bring. The concert performance was very successful, and I received a good deal of praise—but not from my colleagues or the director. In fact, the soaring high I experienced came to a crashing halt a few days later when the music department finally had a meeting to discuss how the concert went. I was attacked for some of the logistical difficulties that were experienced because of the use of so many instruments. Furthermore, I must not have fulfilled my duties because I was asked point blank: "Are you one of us?" That question haunted me. I had to come up with an answer that I could accept so I could get on with doing my job. Sadly, I decided that I was *not* one of them.

I was given total freedom in the implementation of my curriculum, but even then only my failings were sufficiently addressed or recognized. My administrators did not effectively communicate with me, which caused me to have an increasingly negative attitude about the school, the music program, and my colleagues. I began to see only the unsatisfactory or poor qualities of their teaching, performing groups, or personal styles. The initial excitement I felt about that teaching position completely dissipated, and all that was left was a sense of negativity and despair at being unhappy in this new life.

Fortunately, the story doesn't end there. In the early part of the second semester, I tweaked my curriculum, created a controlled and productive learning environment in the classroom, and earned the students' respect. All of this led to a new contract for the next year, the clearest form of approval I could have received. The spring concerts were sensational, and my relations with my coworkers improved. As I look forward to next year, I am glad to have survived another first year.

—Andrew Schulz

Questions for Discussion

- Was there any way Andrew could have been better prepared to teach in this new environment?
- Is it fair to say that learning to teach in such a starkly contrasting environment could never be done satisfactorily at the outset, after one semester, or even after one year?
- How could a mentor have helped in this situation?
- How did the new teacher communicate his or her concerns to the administrators? What may have caused the new teacher to be reluctant to communicate his concerns?
- By choosing to implement his curriculum and not borrow anything from the existing personnel, did the new teacher limit himself from effective input and guidance from colleagues or administrators? By doing his own thing, did he tacitly communicate that he did not want to be part of the department?

The next story addresses issues of teaching many different things in the first year and not always feeling prepared for the variety. This is a concept that is well-documented in general beginning teacher literature, and with P–12 music certification in the majority of states it is very common in music.

The Spackle Effect

Somehow, I've misplaced my job description. I student taught in an elementary general music classroom. I was hired in a very large district with a strong music program and sixteen elementary schools as an elementary general/choral music teacher. It is reassuring to have such a definite title. But somehow that is not exactly what I do. My job has been put together in a piecemeal way since I was hired. I have encountered the "spackle effect."

The spackle effect is the solution often used by administrators to solve their problems, particularly in music. There are very few schools or programs big enough to keep a music teacher of any level in one building all day. As a result, music teachers get divided between buildings in very strange ways to accommodate their district's schedules. A music teacher spends part of his or her week in one building, but then gets sent for twenty-five minutes or an hour to another building or program to fill up a hole in the schedule there. Much like spackling on a wall, this decision fills up the hole, but it does not make the rest of the foundation any more structurally sound. The administrators do this because their hands are tied; they have to fill all scheduled slots with the people they have. They do their best to keep teachers from switching schools and students each year, but sometimes adjustments have to be made based on enrollment.

My degree is actually in instrumental music education. In my undergraduate years, I was on the path to becoming a band director. In my junior year, I decided that I didn't want to be a band director. I spoke to an adviser, who gave me the suggestion that I try elementary music. She was so confident in my abilities that she hired me as a teacher for the university's community music school and assured me that she would help me change my major if I didn't like teaching there. I loved teaching elementary music. I took all elementary music electives, and I was ready to become a general music teacher.

Little did I know how my background would affect me. In my state, all music teachers have the same certification, regardless of their degrees or experiences. Suddenly, during my second year of teaching, holes started to appear in the overall district schedule, and my administrator needed to fill them. I was one of the teachers with the lowest seniority, and I have strong classroom management skills. I also have a very competent supervisor. As positions opened and the budget did not allow him to hire anyone to fill those positions, he came to me. He was very persuasive in telling me that I was just what each position needed. As my ego inflated, so did my schedule.

I have been used to fill more than just elementary general music holes. By my third year of teaching, I was asked to teach middle school chorus for part of my day. I had no choral experience other than my own experiences in high school and teaching one section of fifth grade chorus per week. I spent the whole summer preparing to be in that position only to be told I would be in my original position two weeks before school started. Then in my fourth year I was asked to teach Suzuki violin to kindergarteners. I had never taught or played a string instrument at all (other than in my methods class), and I had no experience with the Suzuki method. Kindergarteners with violins can be very daunting, especially if they threaten to play them. At the end of my fourth year, I was asked to be the assistant band director at the high school as well.

This is a challenge. Just as I feel like I am becoming a proficient teacher in one area, I am sent something new. Sometimes it is very disconcerting to know that I am working at the most basic level. As a first-year teacher, I spent the whole year struggling to keep my head above water. Just as I have begun to feel competent teaching, I have to keep my head above water again in a different area of music. At the same time, the school budgets are getting tighter and tighter, so my schedule includes more teaching in the same length of time. These new tasks are simply added onto what I am already doing. Additionally, I spend a lot of my own money on resources to feel a little more secure in each new area. It is easy to feel overwhelmed and close to burning out.

Although it is hard (and sometimes discouraging) work to try to teach all of these new classes, it has been good for me. I have always been propelled by a personal drive to succeed. I also happen to have a very supportive administrator who has assured me that I would be successful based on the skills that I already have. He shared with me that he picked me for these tasks because he felt that I was up to them, and he knows that I will do a high-quality job with them. I hope he is correct. So far, I've survived. And the spackling is barely noticeable under the paint.

—Regina White Herring

Questions for Discussion

- What will your plan of action be if you are asked to teach outside of your comfortable content area?
- What resources are available in your area to help you in the event that you have to teach a subject area with which you aren't familiar?
- How will you store your methods class information after you begin teaching? Think about how to organize these resources so you can come back to them if you need them.

The final story in this chapter addresses the issue of advocacy for the music program. Research on the careers of music teachers suggests that advocacy for music is one of the beginning teacher concerns that never seems to go away even when a teacher is experienced. Music teachers are always working to garner support. Advocacy is a challenge for beginning music teachers that teachers in other content areas often do not face. Jamal discusses some of the advocacy strategies he used in a large urban school instrumental music program.

Advocacy for Music

Sitting in my undergraduate music education classes, I was told about the role the music educator plays as music advocate. I don't think I fully understood how much of a part advocacy would play in my teaching responsibilities. Throughout my music education, I could only remember one time when the program of the district I attended as a high school student was threatened. As soon as music teachers were rumored to be pink-slipped or programs were supposed to be cut, the community rallied and music programs were saved. I couldn't imagine the role that I would need to play to save a music program.

After four years of public teaching, I have a new perspective. It seems to me that after the responsibility of giving my students a worthwhile and comprehensive experience in music, the next most important role is that of being an advocate for the music program within the community. I must work to ensure that music remains in the students' curriculum. In four years of working in my district, the possibility of reducing or eliminating music programs has been discussed in all but one of those years. Much of my planning is done with a large focus on keeping a program that has integrity and is visible. In those times I have fought to maintain music in the schools.

In a district that has a high degree of building autonomy, the fight for music education is a tough one. In my district, the principal sets the course for what will be offered in his or her building. Outside of core subject areas like math, science, English/language arts, and social studies, there are very few mandates on principals as far as what they will offer in their schools. This means some schools have a very vibrant arts education and some have none. When a principal doesn't support music and the arts, it becomes the educator's job to become an advocate for arts education.

In a time of shrinking budgets, declining enrollment in some districts, and growing accountability, fighting for music programs becomes crucial. When a school is plagued with dropping test scores, it is now held even more accountable, and many non-core classes feel the pressure. In my situation, the response has been for administrators to take students out of elective or encore classes to provide remediation. This takes the music experience away from some students, and depending on the number of students in the situation, it can devastate an ensemble. I have seen situations in which a band went from sixty to thirty. When those numbers were deemed too low to justify the class, twenty beginners were added to this intermediate class.

When my district encountered a multimillion-dollar budget shortfall, arts classes faced problems along with everything else that was deemed "non-essential." School closings, program eliminations and reductions, and teacher layoffs were to be the solutions to this deficit. A building administrator told me that in times like these numbers drive the decisions. The books have to be balanced, and sometimes that means radical positions have to be taken. This is problematic when all involved see that these solutions are not sound. All classes were to be scheduled with the maximum allowable numbers of students per class as far as student enrollment was concerned. Many programs were eliminated and many (including music) were to be reduced. I was very scared for the music program. Up to that point my school had enjoyed a good reputation as far as music was concerned. We were one of only two middle schools in the district that offered band, choir, and orchestra. The other two offered one or two of the three.

As I had seen the writing on the wall from earlier experiences, I decided to always be proactive in advocating for my program. I began to share advocacy materials with anyone who would listen, including my concert audiences. After my group played a few selections, I would cite research done on the benefits of music education. This was probably the most beneficial. The parents were hearing about the benefits of music to students while watching their students perform. The number of other teachers, especially those general classroom teachers, who were very excited and pleased to see that I was making those positive statements about why we need music, also surprised me. At parent-teacher conferences, I shared this information with parents. At teacher meetings, I talked about the benefits of the arts. Music teachers then began taking our concerns to the district-level decision makers. We made the case over and over again as to why music education is important.

When it was all said and done, the campaign had some effects. When the latest rounds of budget cuts were made, they came with some directives from the district. Building principals were told that ALL schools must offer music. The sad part was that band was the only area mandated by the district. Choir and orchestra could be offered at the discretion of the principal. I was happy to see that the district was standing up for music, but it troubled me that all areas were not supported equally.

I believe the reason band programs were saved in this community was in part because of their community visibility. From the high school marching band down to the elementary programs, band directors had been much more proactive in making themselves known. Some band directors were presenting twice as many concerts as their choir and orchestra colleagues. This allowed the bands to always be in the limelight. The band directors were much better at getting the band performances on district television and in other media. Band programs were simply more visible than any other program. It can be hard for someone to cut a program they view as essential. I think when we try to make our programs more visible, all students benefit. The act of performing allows the students to showcase their talents and gives them something to be proud of. It also makes others aware of our achievements. The other teachers have standardized tests to show student achievement or lack thereof, and performance is the way music teachers must show this achievement. When it is all said and done we have to teach with drive and passion. We have to advocate as if the future of our children depends on it—because it does.

—Jamal Duncan

Questions for Discussion

- What is the appropriate place of music education in the entire curriculum of a student?
- How do you plan to serve as the face of your music program as well as an advocate for music education?
- What is the difference between music education and entertainment? How do you distinguish between those in an educational setting?
- What are some ways to make music education attractive to students without jeopardizing the integrity of the subject? (Because music education programs are seen in many schools as elective or encore, this is something we must think about.)

Chapter Eleven
Mentoring

Positive mentor relationships are one of the keys to addressing the myriad challenges documented in Chapters Nine and Ten. The first step in seeking the best mentor help is to search for information regarding state and district mentor policies. Most states now have some sort of required mentor program for beginning music teachers. The 2003 MENC publication *Great Beginnings for Music Teachers: Mentoring and Supporting New Teachers* provides a state-by-state overview of mentor policies in place in 2003. The state education Web site for any state usually has information about what a first-year teacher should expect. Many state music organizations also describe mentor programs on their Web sites. Sometimes a school district will be able to provide a music teacher as a mentor, but in other cases the official assigned mentor for a music teacher may be another teacher in the building. Beginning music teachers must learn how to use the non-music mentor in a valuable way, and if no music mentor is assigned, the teacher must seek a music content-area mentor on his or her own. The more mentors the beginning teacher has, the better.

Because you will most likely have both non-music and music mentors, we try to present mentor interaction guidelines that work for all types of mentors. A new teacher must be proactive in getting one or more mentors. Administrators may or may not facilitate this pairing.

Finding a Mentor

Right after you get your first job, begin to seek a variety of mentors you can call on even before you need them. Regardless of what the district provides or sets up for you, seek someone in your building as well as several music mentors. If there is no other music teacher in your building ask the principal for a recommendation regarding whom else to contact. Try to have at least one mentor lined up before the first day of school so you can talk through issues for the first day. For many music teachers what might be considered the "first day of school" is often in the summer at band camp or some other some musical activity. Research has documented that it is during these first few student and parent interactions that new music teachers need mentor support. Be sure you are prepared with your support system.

Don't be shy in contacting someone you may never have met and asking him or her to be on call for questions you might have about teaching music. In addition, try to meet with your mentors early on in the year so you can get to know them as people and as teachers before you need them in more formal roles. Remember that even a very experienced mentor was once a beginning teacher, and most mentors really do want to help. Most teachers struggle with the challenges documented in Chapter Nine, so don't be embarrassed when you have difficulties, and don't be afraid to ask for help.

Research on mentoring in music has suggested that, in addition to having an experienced mentor, many beginning music teachers find mentoring from second- or third-year teachers helpful as well. If there is a new music teacher who has just a few years of music teaching in your area, you might consider regular meetings with that person. Research has also suggested that the age of children the mentor teaches can be as important as the musical content. For example, if you are teaching middle school band you may find the middle school choral music teacher as valuable as the high school band teacher because questions you have relate specifically to the age of the children.

Most music teachers find the informal interactions they have with other music teachers at conferences and rehearsals to be the most valuable source of professional development. Don't wait for a conference or rehearsal to take advantage of this resource. I have worked with several groups of beginning music teachers who meet every Friday after school to download from the week, and they often report this as the best type of mentoring they have.

Characteristics of Mentors

Building a relationship with a mentor is much like any other sort of relationship. No one person is going to have all the characteristics you might value in a mentor. Some teachers make good mentors, while others are good with children but not good in working with adults (which is essentially what mentoring is). Each of the criteria listed below is discussed in relation to how the beginning music teacher might consider each characteristic. The list was derived from research on what beginning music teachers say they look for in a mentor. Some of these characteristics will not be important to you (although they were important to someone else). The beginning teacher should examine what they are looking for or expecting from the mentor.

Excellent musician. Because many beginning music teachers are just coming from a teacher education program in a school or department of music, we have found they often desire a music mentor that they consider to be an excellent musician. What the beginning teacher must remember is how this is defined for a veteran music teacher. Many music teachers are still actively involved as performing musicians, but others model their musicianship from the podium or in other ways. Be careful not to make snap judgments regarding a mentor based on his or her applied performance work. Musicianship for a music teacher evolves over his or her career. Try to examine how the music mentor defines his or her musicianship, and broaden your understanding of the field.

Strong knowledge of subject matter. The music mentor must have a strong knowledge of the music content. Once again, this definition may be different for the beginning music teacher than for the mentor. Although you may be able to rattle off details from music theory or music history class, you may find that what the mentor knows (and what you need to know) is how to teach the subject matter. A non-music mentor will obviously not have subject-area knowledge in music. However, his or her knowledge of how children learn in another subject area may be quite helpful to you if you can phrase your questions in a general context.

Exemplary teacher. Being an exemplary teacher has been documented as an important criterion for a mentor. Even a non-music mentor who is an exemplary teacher can be perceived as helpful to beginning music teachers. An exemplary teacher (in any content area) is able to motivate students while providing developmentally appropriate instruction and empowering students to guide their own learning. Exemplary teachers talk about teaching and learning in a passionate way and are always ready to try new ways of reaching students. There are many exemplary teachers in every school building. Students in the building will know who they are. Seek out those teachers for assistance and guidance whether they are your assigned mentors or not.

Similar philosophy of music education. Some new teachers have been prepared with quite specific methodologies and ideas regarding music teaching and learning. Some mentors go into a mentoring relationship with the thought that they may have the opportunity to learn about new ways of teaching music that the beginning teacher may bring. Others have their tried and true way of teaching and want the mentee to embrace it. Mentees are often the same. Some come into the teaching situation ready to learn other ways of teaching music, and others believe that the way they learned in their college or university is the "best" or maybe the "only" way. Both the music mentor and the mentee must be open-minded and flexible if the relationship is to be successful. Of course, just as in any relationship, the issues of philosophical differences may be so great that no healthy growth can occur. This is why it is important to seek a variety of mentors.

Proactive in establishing a relationship. Successful mentor relationships are a two-way street in terms of communication. Even if you are a beginning teacher who has been proactive in finding your mentors, you will want a mentor who is also proactive in keeping in touch with you. When school gets going and you get busy you will need that person "knocking on your door." This is true for both music and non-music mentors.

Good listener. Being a good listener has been defined as one of the important characteristics of a mentor. Sometimes you, as the beginning teacher, just need to talk about what has happened in the classroom. You may not be looking for feedback and suggestions. It is important to find someone (who could even be a spouse or family member) who can just let you talk.

Organized. Some beginning teachers have suggested that the mentor must be organized. If the beginning teacher is a very organized person, then he or she wants a mentor who is the same way. Again, how one defines organized can affect the relationship match. Many music teachers are very organized, but they still may have a stack of papers on their desks. We believe the need for this concept of organization is closely related to the next category of "strong knowledge of policies and procedures."

Strong knowledge of policies and procedures (building, district, and state). Music teachers need mentors who can help them with the paperwork required by the job. You may need to seek multiple mentors who understand these issues at the building, school district, and state level. A close relationship with a secretary or other district personnel who really know the details of the paperwork is a must.

Personable but professional. This final characteristic is again related to a personality match between mentor and mentee. Finding a comfortable balance between being personable yet professional is important. Some beginning music teachers want a mentor who will support them in life as well as music teaching, and others seek a music mentor only and rely on family and friends for other sorts of support. Beginning music teachers should be clear about the level and type of mentor support they seek.

As you look back over the list of criteria, it is important to target those elements a non-music mentor may be able to provide. Although they may not know the music content, an exemplary teacher may be helpful in a variety of other ways. It is useful for the music teacher to have support and contacts from teachers in other content areas. A non-music mentor can help the music teacher make these contacts.

Observation

Whether or not the mentor is a music teacher, one of the most important elements of successful mentoring is that the mentor be able to observe the beginning teacher in the classroom. Although the beginning teacher may feel nervous about inviting an experienced teacher into the classroom, it is absolutely crucial that the mentor have a sense of the teaching context. The beginning teacher might start the year by observing the mentor in the mentor's classroom first. Then the mentor might come to the beginner's classroom and do some teaching. Depending on the teaching context, some team teaching may be appropriate. It is important for you to feel comfortable inviting the mentor or mentors in to help.

When you invite the mentor into your classroom, let your students know that the mentor is coming and will be helping you in your work as a teacher. Introduce the mentor to your students when he or she arrives. If possible, try to meet with your mentor in advance of the observation, and have a discussion regarding what you would like for them to see and react to. The Mentor Interaction Guide at the end of the chapter includes questions for the pre-observation and post-observation meeting between mentor and mentee. If possible, videotape the observation so you and the mentor can view the classroom together. Invite the mentor to observe often, and he or she will have a better sense of your classroom and be able to help you more.

Logistics

Sometimes mentors and mentees are required to meet and document their conversations. In other settings the mentor-mentee interaction is more informal. Mentors and mentees who have regularly scheduled interactions (whether formal or informal) perceive the relationship as more valuable. In some settings mentors are prepared for their roles through professional development offerings, and in other settings no preparation is provided. The same is true for paying a stipend to mentors. In some cases a mentor is paid a stipend for the work with the mentee and in other cases not. The school provides payment for the mentor. Mentors who are prepared for their roles are usually more successful. Also, if they are paid even a small amount for their work, they feel a greater responsibility to assist the beginning teacher. As a beginning teacher, you will not have control of most of these factors. However, you can be proactive about regular meetings even if your mentor is not paid or trained for his or her role.

Comments from Beginning Music Teachers Regarding Mentoring

The two short quotes included here remind beginning music teachers that they must take responsibility for making mentoring work. Experienced teachers should take some responsibility too, but the beginning teacher who is proactive will have more mentor relationship success.

> Find a mentor ASAP. If the one assigned by the school isn't helpful, then find a good one on your own. I can't even count how many times I have gone to my mentor asking him to tell me for the zillionth time why I need to be a teacher, reassure me that I'm not going insane, advise me how to deal with administrators, and to soak my head when I've had a bad day. Share the victories as well as the battles with your mentor so that you're not constantly dumping on them, and so that they can be reminded of when they were just starting out and a student did something right for the first time (Conway and Garlock, 2002).
>
> —Mandi Garlock, elementary general music teacher

> It was incredibly helpful to have a mentor who did essentially the same job I was doing. Most of my questions were about things he had experienced, so he was readily able to guide me when I needed it. He was also able to remind me when deadlines were coming up for festival applications, dues, etc., because his deadlines were the same. Although he would have helped me in this capacity regardless, it did help that the district trained and paid its mentors a nominal stipend. We were expected to meet for an hour once a month (although we were allowed to count some of our e-mail time). At these meetings he was able to help me in a variety of ways, such as looking at my festival music, helping me decide if I had overprogrammed my eighth graders (I had), and going through the mountains of percussion accessories my predecessor had amassed to help me decide what was usable and what was not.
>
> Some would argue that there is an inherent problem in not having a mentor within the building. I grant there were building-specific questions I needed answered. It would have been nice to have someone in the building who could observe my teaching on his or her planning period. This is where it is necessary to do what is best for yourself, your program, and your students. I spent nearly as much time asking questions of the

secretaries and custodians as I did of my mentor. It can be intimidating being a newcomer to the building, but most of the rest of the staff would like to see you succeed!

Again, I was very fortunate that circumstances turned out as they did for me. I like to think that if things had been different, I would have had the courage to seek assistance wherever I could get it—from veteran teachers, state organization members, former professors, and even my own former band directors. Even when I felt fairly certain about my own decisions, it was always reassuring to be able to bounce them off of someone experienced. I hope that someday I will be able to provide that same assistance to a young teacher (Conway and Zerman, 2004).

—Tavia Zerman, middle school band director

This chapter concludes with a guide for mentor-mentee interactions. Some of the issues cannot be addressed with some mentors (e.g., musical questions for a non-music mentor or building issues for a non-building mentor). Use the guide as a resource for finding the right help as well.

Mentor Interaction Guide

First Meeting (as soon as you take the job and can secure the mentor)

- Ask your mentor teacher to tell you a bit about his or her career and work. How long has he or she been teaching? At what levels? In what types of communities?
- Ask your mentor to discuss the aspects of their teaching that they work on the hardest in their own teaching? What types of issues in teaching are they still curious about? What do they struggle with?
- Ask your mentor to discuss why they are interested in being a mentor. Discuss the parameters of the relationship. You may want to decide that all interactions between the two of you are to be kept confidential so that you both feel comfortable talking about whatever needs to be addressed.
- Ask your mentor for tips on allocating and managing the music budget for your area. He or she may be aware of expenses you had not considered.
- Discuss choosing literature if you are an ensemble teacher, and try to get some suggestions for tried and true literature for your ensemble. Get some assistance in ordering the music or materials.

Meeting Right before School Starts

- Go over your plans for the first day of school (or band camp or whatever your first interaction with students may be) with your mentor. Consider carefully any suggestions or advice they may have.
- Talk about classroom procedures and rules. Tell your mentor how you plan to set up the classroom, and get their thoughts and feedback.
- Ask about paperwork for music organizations (registrations, etc.) that you may not know about because you are new. Again, you may need to find a mentor from within the state music organization to meet this need.
- Ask your mentor to call or e-mail you every time he or she completes some sort of administrative task for the job (e.g., bus requests for solo and ensemble contests). Then you can be reminded of these deadlines as well. A music mentor is needed for this.
- Make arrangements to go observe the mentor in his or her teaching setting as soon as possible. Even if the mentor is not teaching music this can be a useful way to get a sense of how the mentor views teaching and learning.
- Discuss how and when the mentor can come and observe you.
- Make a schedule for weekly (if possible) meetings.

Weekly Meetings

- Begin each weekly meeting with a focus on the positive events from the week. What do you think is going well?
- No question is too basic for your mentor. Keep a list all week of questions and concerns to run by him or her.
- Share weekly and monthly goals with your mentor so he or she can help you to prioritize.
- Topics that beginning music teachers in the past have suggested are useful to discuss include working with parents, classroom management, planning instruction and choosing literature, building and maintaining rapport with students, working with administrators, assessment and grading, administrative organization of the music program, and overall getting-to-know-you issues in the school district. You might try to limit your meetings to one or two topics each meeting so there is time to really address the issue in depth.

- Be proactive in telling your mentor what you need from him or her. Ask to be observed as this is often the most useful interaction between the mentor and mentee.
- End each weekly meeting with a strategy for growth for the week. Share with your mentor how you will attempt to attain and measure this goal.

Meeting before an Observation

- How do you want the mentor to help?
- What would you like them to notice?
- What would you like them to document? You might ask them to just script every word that you say. Or you might ask them to describe the entire room or to document the responses of a few students or a section.
- What do you expect will be the challenges on that day? Let the mentor know that in advance.
- Do you want the mentor's thoughts regarding improvement? Or do you want them just to describe what they see?
- Discuss where the mentor will sit in the room. Will he or she participate in the musical activity? Sit in the back of the room? Sit in the front? You decide what would make you most comfortable.

Meeting after the Observation

- Begin with a discussion of what you think went well in that lesson or rehearsal.
- Share your concerns from that day with your mentor.
- If you are comfortable, ask the mentor for his or her suggestions for improvement. Based on the suggestions, create your own strategies for meeting future goals.

Chapter Twelve
Professional Development Support

Most states require continued professional development for teachers to maintain certification. Information regarding required professional development is usually available on the state education Web site. Many states now have professional development programs specifically for beginning teachers. These programs are often referred to as "induction" programs. Although most states have some sort of induction program policy, there is great variation from the national perspective regarding these policies for beginning teachers. A few states have state-level beginning teacher programs (e.g., the BTSA—Beginning Teacher Support and Assessment program in California and the BEST—Beginning Educator Support and Training program in Connecticut). Some areas of the country have regional beginning teacher programs where several school districts pool their resources and provide a beginning teacher program. These large-scale state and regional programs often include teacher in-service days and mentor support. They are sometimes able to provide music, content-specific in-service and mentoring.

Many of the national variations in programs are related to funding. In a majority of states, funding for beginning teacher programs is left to local level initiatives. For the most part, wealthier suburban districts often have detailed beginning teacher programs while other types of districts do not. These wealthier districts often provide professional development workshops specific to beginning teacher needs and a trained mentor who is paid for his or her work. In districts that cannot provide such support, the beginning teacher is left on his or her own to secure appropriate professional development as well as mentor support. Even in the most well supported state, regional, or local program, professional development classes and workshops are often not music-content related.

The first step in creating a good experience is to recognize the inability of many school districts to provide content-related professional development support. Lack of resources (funds as well as participants and presenters) makes it difficult for many induction programs to include content-specific professional development. You will most likely need to look outside the district for programs that provide you with music-specific support.

211

Survival Strategies versus Professional Development

Connecting generic induction programs to the music content area and securing music content support is only one of the challenges of induction. Another challenge is the nature of induction itself. It has been our experience that beginning music teachers are often inducted into a school by being provided with "this is how it works around here" information. This comes from administrators, parents, and students just as often as it comes from other teachers. Formal induction programs sometimes show the same attitude. We worry that in our effort to support you as beginning music teachers we may be robbing you of the opportunity to make changes both inside the profession and in society at large. Although you have not been in a situation to try out your ideas in teaching practice, many of your have graduated from preservice programs with some ideas regarding music teaching and learning. If your only experiences with colleagues in early professional development programs center around meeting the status quo, then the profession loses the opportunity to continue improving music teaching and learning.

Beginning music teachers should know that the profession is just beginning to focus on valuing what you bring to a school. Mentor programs that include training and development for the mentors now focus on the mentor learning how to empower the beginning teacher to grow and share his or her ideas. However, in many settings you may still be made to feel as though your opinions don't matter. You must combat these feelings by surrounding yourself with colleagues and professionals who are interested in collaborative discussions about teaching and learning. Seek professional development options that allow you to participate and share your ideas. These interactions help you get beyond surviving the first year and move toward real growth as a teacher.

Many music induction programs (even the ones presented by music organizations) are presented to beginning teachers as survival sessions. Session titles we have seen include "Music Teachers Survival Camp," "What They Didn't Teach You in College about Being a Music Teacher," "Strategies for Getting through the First Year," "Everything You Need to Survive That First Year as a Music Teacher." Although some of the tips you gather at these types of workshops may be helpful for some nitty-gritty issues in the short term, if your beginning music teacher professional development is seen as a first-year survival program, then the kind of effect that the program can have on real teacher growth is minimal. This is not to say that music teacher strategies for survival should be removed from your experience. However, all of us in the profession must recognize that merely presenting short-term survival strategies is not enough.

What You Can Do

Because much of what may be provided to you by state, local, district, and even music organization-sponsored professional development initiatives may or may not be useful to your growth as a beginning teacher, be prepared to find help on your own. If you need more information on some area of your music job, arrange to take a course or go to a workshop, and then advocate using that as professional development. The table below includes a variety of ideas for music professional development. Ask your building principal if you can participate in some of these activities and count them as professional development. Or ask your mentor to help you in advocating for these types of professional development activities in your school.

Professional Development Ideas

- Visit the classroom of another music teacher working in an area in which you feel you need more help. Spend the day observing and speaking with them about their work.
- Invite an experienced music teacher to your classroom for a series of workshops with your students. Take notes and get new ideas for working with your students from these mentors.
- Shadow some of your most difficult students as they work with other teachers in the building so you can see how they interact in other settings.
- Observe the most well respected teacher at the school regardless of the content area to get a sense of what makes that teacher so successful.
- Invite a university professor to your class to observe and give you feedback.
- Conduct an action research study in your classroom to examine something you want to know more about.
- Create an inquiry group of beginning teachers in the building or district (music and non-music), and arrange to meet regularly to talk about beginning teacher issues.
- Create an inquiry group of local music teachers who arrange to meet regularly to talk about music teaching and learning.

With the right kind of documentation, we have seen all of these options approved as professional development in school.

Keeping a reflective journal or diary may help you to reflect upon past teaching experiences and learn from them. Many induction programs require this

213

sort of record keeping. Even if you are not participating in a program that encourages journaling, consider even using an informal journal to document your teaching experiences and thoughts about your work. Try to write a few comments each week regarding what you think is going well and what you want to work on. Some of the reflection tools from early in this book may take on new usefulness once you are in a job and working every day.

Ongoing Professional Development

Many states recognize that the period of growth for a beginning teacher goes beyond the first year. However, beginning teacher programs are primarily geared toward the first year. As you move into your second, third, and fourth year, issues that go beyond survival often trouble you. All good teachers know that learning to teach is a career-long endeavor. However, many teachers quit the profession in the first five years due to frustration.

Some beginning teachers don't ask questions about improving themselves and their classrooms. Some of these teachers get through the survival stage of the first year and settle into a "teaching groove" that works for them. It is hard to watch beginning teachers teach their second year for the rest of their career. These teachers mean well, they like the students, and they try to make connections for students. However, they lack the reflective capacity to continue to grow. Be proactive in finding continued support into the second and third year of teaching.

Teacher Evaluation, Professional Development Credits, and Permanent Licensure

Most states have some time period considered the induction phase in which a teacher holds a provisional teaching certificate. This time period is usually somewhere between two and five years. After the induction period teachers can apply for and receive a more permanent certificate. In some states a teacher must have a master's degree in order to obtain a permanent license. In others, a certain number of university courses and/or professional development credits are required. The state education Web site for each state has information regarding permanent licensure. Beginning teachers should take it upon themselves to be aware of the state licensure policies. Some school districts are careful to provide this information in beginning teacher induction programs while others leave it completely up to the teacher to meet state requirements. Take extra care to understand the timeline in your state. If you have to complete a master's degree, how long do you have? Does the degree have to be completed or started in a certain time period? The responsibility for the documentation of professional development ultimately rests on the beginning teacher. Even a mentor is not always a good source of information about these policies as the policies may have changed since the mentor was hired.

Be aware of state and district policies regarding teacher evaluation. Who will complete your annual teaching performance review? In many cases, it is the building principal. Sometimes it may be an assistant principal. Some states have state-level teacher evaluators. In some states mentors are hired to be evaluators. This is a sticky issue as most people in the profession believe that for mentoring to work there should be no evaluative relationship. However, some are still exploring the mentor and evaluator mix. The bottom line is that the beginning teacher must search to know who is doing what and whom to go to for help and assistance.

Professional Memberships

Another source of development can be membership in one of the many professional music organizations. These groups often sponsor professional development workshops and mentoring programs, and they often provide Web-based and print magazines, articles, and materials. The list in this chapter is not comprehensive but provides links to many of the most well known national professional music organizations. There may be other local music organizations in your state or community.

> **Music Educators National Conference:** www.menc.org
> **American String Teacher's Association:** www.astaweb.com
> **American Choral Director's Association:** www.acdaonline.org
> **American School Band Director's Association:**
> home.comcast.net/~asbda
> **Midwest Band and Orchestra Clinic:**
> www.midwestclinic.org/conferenceinfo.asp
> **Gordon Institute for Music Learning:** www.giml.org
> **American Orff-Schulwerk Association:** www.aosa.org
> **Organization of American Kodály Educators:** www.oake.org

It may be possible to attend clinics and workshops sponsored by any of these organizations and to apply for professional development or graduate credit for your participation in these events. Always check with the school district regarding whether the district will honor certain types of professional development options.

Graduate School

We get many questions from young teachers regarding the options for graduate school. In states that require a master's degree for permanent certification, the degree itself is usually not dictated by the state. In other words, music teachers could get a degree in music education, but they could also do graduate work in performance, conducting, theory, musicology, general education, psychology, educational administration, or any other field.

Beginning teachers working in states that require a degree must be proactive in understanding the state requirements in terms of time and degree completion. Many music teachers opt to complete a master's degree in a summer program so they are able to keep teaching while they are in school. There are a variety of programs in music education and conducting that can be completed in the summer. Performance, theory, or musicology degrees usually require a school-year residency (of course, there are exceptions to everything).

Degrees in a college of education (general education, psychology, and in some cases music education) are often designed for practicing teachers and can be completed in the evenings and on weekends. Some programs can be started right away, and others require a prerequisite number of years of teaching before entry into the program. Graduate school is almost always considered appropriate professional development by district, local, and state licensure policy boards.

Checklist for Beginning Teachers Regarding Professional Development

- Do you know the policy regarding professional development in your school district and in your state? (In some instances these may be different from one another.)
- Do you know how to document your professional development, to whom you submit these materials, and when?
- Do you know who will provide your professional evaluations?
- Are you a member of one of the professional organizations that can provide music content-related professional development?
- Have you gathered resources on professional development workshops that are relevant to your music classroom needs?

Research Base for the First Years as a Music Teacher

Bowles, C. 2003. The self-expressed professional development needs of music educators. *Update: Applications of Research in Music Education* 21(1): 24–28.

Conway, C. M. 2001. Beginning music teacher perceptions of district-sponsored induction programs. *Bulletin of the Council for Research in Music Education* 151: 51–62.

———. 2001. What has research told us about the beginning music teacher? *Journal of Music Teacher Education* 10(2): 14–22.

———. 2003. An examination of district-sponsored beginning music teacher mentor practices. *Journal of Research in Music Education* 51(1): 372–391.

Conway, C. M., D. Albert, S. Hibbard, and R. Hourigan. 2005. Arts education and professional development. *Arts Education Policy Review* 107(1): 3–9.

———. 2005. Voices of music teachers regarding professional development. *Arts Education Policy Review* 107(1): 11–14.

Conway, C. M., and J. A. Borst. 2001. Action research in music education. *Update: Applications of Research in Music Education* 19(2): 3–8.

Conway, C. M., and T. Jeffers. 2004. The teacher as researcher in beginning instrumental music. *Update: Applications of Research in Music Education* 22(2): 35–45.

Conway, C. M., P. Krueger, M. Robinson, P. Haack, and M. V. Smith. 2002. Beginning music teacher mentor and induction policy: A cross-state perspective. *Arts Education Policy Review* 104(2): 9–17.

Conway, C. M., and T. E. H. Zerman. 2004. Perceptions of an instrumental music teacher regarding mentoring, induction, and the first year of teaching. *Research Studies in Music Education* 22: 72–82.

DeLorenzo, L. 1992. Perceived problems of beginning music teachers. *Bulletin of the Council for Research in Music Education* 113: 9–25.

Feiman-Nemser, S. 1993. *Teacher mentoring: A critical review.* ERIC Clearinghouse on Teaching and Teacher Education.

Feiman-Nemser, S., S. Schwille, C. Carver, and B. Yusko. 1999. *A conceptual review of literature on new teacher induction. National partnership of excellence and accountability in teaching.* East Lansing, Michigan: NPEAT.

Jones, G. S. 1978. A descriptive study of problems encountered by first-year instrumental teachers in Oregon. PhD diss., University of Oregon.

Krueger, P. J. 1996. Becoming a music teacher: Challenges of the first year. *Dialogue in Instrumental Music* 20(2): 88–104.

———. 1999. New music teachers speak out on mentoring. *Journal of Music Teacher Education* 8: 7–13.

Montague, M. G. 2000. Processes and situatedness: A collective case study of selected mentored music teachers. PhD diss., University of Oregon.

Smith, M. V. 1994. The mentoring and development of new music educators: A descriptive study of a pilot program. PhD diss., University of Minnesota.

Suggested Reading for the First Years as a Music Teacher

Conway, C. M., ed. 2003. *Great beginnings for music teachers: Mentoring and supporting new teachers*. Reston, VA: MENC.

Conway, C. M., E. Hansen, A. Schulz, J. Stimson, and J. Wozniak. 2004. Becoming a music teacher: Voices of the first three years. *Music Educators Journal* 91(1): 4–52.

Kane, P. R., ed. *The first year of teaching*. New York: Walker and Company.

Kronowitz, E. L. 2004. *Your first year of teaching and beyond*. 4th ed. Boston: Pearson.

Krueger, P. J. 2001. Reflections of beginning music teachers. *Music Educators Journal* 88(3): 51–54.

Music Educators National Conference. 2002. *Teacher success kit*. Reston, VA: MENC.

———. 2004. Are there any mentors out there? In *Spotlight on transition to teaching music*. Reston, VA: MENC.

———. 2004. How can you survive your first years of teaching? In *Spotlight on transition to teaching music*. Reston, VA: MENC.

Roehrig, A. D., M. Pressley, and D. Talotta. 2002. *Stories of beginning teachers*. Notre Dame, IN: University of Notre Dame Press.

Scherer, M., ed. 1999. *A better beginning: Supporting and mentoring new teachers*. Alexandria, VA: Association for Supervision and Curriculum Development.

Shieh, E., and C. M. Conway. 2004. Professional induction: Programs and policies for beginning teachers. In *Questioning the music education paradigm, Vol. 2*, ed. L. Bartel, 162–178. Toronto: Canadian Music Educators Association.

Wilke, R. L. 2003. *The first days of class–A practical guide for the beginning teacher*. Thousand Oaks, CA: Corwin.

Wong, H. K., and R. T. Wong. 1998. *The first days of school*. Mountain View, CA: Harry K. Wong Publications.

Online Discussion Forums for Beginning Music Teachers

MENC: The National Association for Music Education forums (www.menc.org): Discussions of teaching tips, new ideas, reform issues, and more, including specific forums for band, orchestra, chorus, and general music teachers. The "Ask the Mentors" link is particularly useful.

Music Teacher Chatboard (teachers.net/mentors/music): Gateway to music resources on the Internet and mentor support center for music teachers.

National Board for Professional Teaching Standards (NBPTS) Music Discussion Group (groups.yahoo.com/group/NBPTSmusic).
Subscribe at: NBPTSmusic subscribe@yahoogroups.com.
Post messages at: NBPTSmusic@yahoogroups.com. This is a discussion group for music teachers going through the National Board certification process, but it is open to anyone.

Epilogue
What Keeps Them Going?

We hope the following five stories from beginning teachers who responded to the question "What keeps you going?" will inspire and encourage you.

Jarod: A Reflection on Student Teaching

When Jarod came into the music room, he was already pretty worked up and angry. It appeared that he and some of the other second grade boys were pushing each other in their line. As Ms. Morris quieted the students for class, she had to remind them, "Please don't address your teacher with 'Hey.'" At this, Jarod began (loudly) lamenting the inequity of the respect teachers show students versus the respect students owe teachers. Then—I only realized after the fact—he pushed Ms. Morris from behind. She was surprised, of course, but the first words out of her mouth were: "Jarod, are you having a bad day?" He said "yes" and "yes" again when she asked whether he was going to continue having a bad day in music class. So she sent him to spend the class period at a table by the door.

For the first twenty minutes of class, Jarod was intentionally as obnoxious as he could be. He wandered from his table and yelled the rhythmic echoes of the day's lesson at all the wrong times. Several times, Ms. Morris had to tell him to go back to his seat by the door. I also had to reprimand him multiple times; once he appeared to be eating paper towels (he informed me that he needed to be able to chew on something); a couple of other times he was standing on the chair or on the table. But...gradually...he began to mellow out. He folded his arms on the table and put his head down. It was about this time that he also started asking me if he could rejoin the class. I knew he could not and told him so. A

219

girl (possibly his sister) appeared at Ms. Morris's door with his glasses. Jarod put them on and whispered, "Now that I have my glasses, I can be good. Can I go back to class?" He seemed so sad.

When class was over, Ms. Morris told Jarod to wait with me while she walked the other students back to their homeroom. I had him move over to a chair by my desk near an off-kilter rolling rack of music stands. He began sort of hanging on this rack, so I said, "Jarod, let go. I'm going to move these so you don't hurt yourself." He answered, "I want to hurt myself." After two more unsuccessful attempts to make him let go, I warned him that I was going to count to three. He let go. I moved the stands, but when I turned back around, Jarod was hitting his head on a stack of chairs. Perhaps this was to prove his intention to hurt himself.

I pulled his chair over to my desk away from the stack and said, "Jarod, tell me about your day." He looked at the ground, mumbled, and hemmed and hawed. Finally, he told me that he was having a bad day because he hadn't taken his medication that morning. He had forgotten, and his auntie had forgotten, so all day long he had been getting in trouble. He said that one of his classmates had kicked him, and Jarod had pushed back. He spoke about other similar incidents, but it was hard to make out his words because he was speaking very softly.

I attempted to swing the conversation in a more positive direction by asking Jarod what he liked about school. He said he disliked all of it, except recess. He asked in a very frightened and low voice, "Am I going to be sent to Mr. Orland's office?" The question made me wince slightly. I knew that Mr. Orland, the assistant principal, had a reputation among the teachers as being overly harsh with troublemakers. I also knew Ms. Morris avoided sending kids to him at all costs, but I wasn't sure how angry she was over Jarod's act of aggression and irritating behavior. I looked at the little boy before me and said with heartfelt emotion, "I hope not."

Something about our interactions began to remind me of the men I had met a few months earlier when I was helping to lead a music workshop at Parnall Correctional Facility. Perhaps it was the way that Jarod, like the inmates, was such a wonderfully pleasant person to be around one on one. I felt that he was a victim of circumstances. It seemed he had very few opportunities to talk to someone who cared about him. Were it not for the fact that I happened to be there as a second teacher in Ms. Morris's room, he probably would have gone through the whole school day without one person understanding why he was having so many emotional outbursts. It was so frustrating. I know teachers have to discipline students according to their actions because they are visible, but it seems as though there is just never the time or the opportunity in a school day to *talk* with students and figure out what's going on. This problem is exacerbated in urban schools like Jarod's, where school psychologists and social workers are in high demand and short supply. I imagined Jarod growing up with many, many other days like this one and no one to understand him. It was too much.

Jarod noticed the tears slipping down my cheeks. He softly asked, "You all right, Ms. Strasser?" Not surprisingly, his innocent and compassionate question made it even more difficult for me to keep my emotions under control, so I invited him to draw pictures with me to distract us both. Ms. Morris returned while we were drawing. She had dispelled all of her anger on her walk back to the performing arts wing. After a few firm but kind words to Jarod, she walked him back to class. I, in turn, left the school building for a few minutes to walk around the block and regain my composure. I had little success. The ugly apartments I passed were forceful reminders of the huge inequalities in our society. Why must children like Jarod grow up in this clamor? There is no answer, of course—just a renewed desire to work toward change.

—Diane Strasser Platte

Teaching Community

For the third time this year, the custodian who looks after my hallway has changed, and I go over to say hello. Her name is Margaret, and she's about sixty-five-years-old. She tells me I have the worst job in the world. "My grandson is going to be a history teacher," she says. "That's fantastic!" I say. "I think it's awful," she replies. "Really awful."

She is referring to the disrespect, the thanklessness, and the seeming ineffectiveness of the teaching—the part of the job that makes her say "kids these days." To me, that is the reason for my job. I teach orchestra at a low-income urban middle school and high school in St. Louis, Missouri, where my daily struggle is to make music from and in chaos. Somewhere during that struggle, I am convinced, is the possibility of creating community, something "kids these days" seem to experience less and less frequently and something I believe can have a far-reaching effect. Nonetheless, with the suspension list more than three times as long now as it was at the beginning of the year, the building staff and I are beginning to wonder whether anything good has come out of all the work we have done.

Two members of my eighth grade orchestra are on that suspension list, and a colleague once observed that my eighth graders must be the most delinquent group of students ever placed together in a classroom. These students gave me no beginning-of-school honeymoon period: on the first day, almost all the students walked in anywhere from three to thirty minutes late. On the second day, two of them got into a fistfight. In the third week, Destiny proclaimed she wouldn't play Elliot Del Borgo's *Fantasia on Amazing Grace* and continued to throw tantrums for the rest of the semester when asked to take out her instrument.

At the beginning of the school year, the orchestra simply could not function. The students refused to find a common goal in creating music, and in that general atmosphere of apathy and antagonism, there was no desire to work as a group. Many of my colleagues urged me to get tough and punish the students with the detentions and suspensions the students had learned to expect from other teachers. However, though this certainly would have brought them in line, it would have ended any possibility of building community, and I doubted if I could bear creating music through coercion. While I tried various tactics over the course of the first few months to bring students on board, inevitably I waited.

Thankfully, one of the great benefits of a musical ensemble is that it has performances. In December the eighth graders were surprised to find themselves outplayed by the sixth grade orchestra. They came back in January embarrassed, angry, and, for the first time, united by a common purpose: not to be out-played. Students began to police each other: "Be quiet Deandra! Mr. Shieh is trying to help us sound good." The fights slowly eased up, the instruments came out of their cases, and somehow playing became *fun*. One day in May the students were able to plan and execute a very productive rehearsal while I sat in the back.

A large part of teaching community has been encouraging individuals to take responsibility for their parts—responsibility that is often returned in full by the rest of the group. At a first-year teacher workshop I shared the story of Phil, my eighth grade bass player. Phil likes to knock out backbeats on his bass, and in fact that was all he did at the beginning of the year. Any attempt to get him to play resulted in his sitting down and glaring at me. "Why you ask me to play? They ain't doing nothin'," he would say, referring to the rest of the class. Not to mention his standard remark: "That's so gay."

After about a month of this, I gave Phil a shock to his system. I pulled him into my office after class and told him he was incredibly talented. "Your beats are amazing," I said, "and I know your bass playing could be too." And before he could reply, I had called his mother and was telling her how talented her son was and how *that night* I was going to bring the school's only other bass to her home so he could practice. Both mother and son were speechless.

By November, Phil had started working in class. One day he came in and said proudly, "Last night I practiced *and* I did my math homework." His math teacher was shocked. By January, he was pushing other students to get their acts together, and in February he was accepted into a citywide honors orchestra and was overawed to find himself in an orchestra with seven other bassists. In March he stopped using the words "that's so gay" in class and would instead say, "That's so—I'm not going to say it."

Right before a performance at the end of the year, I said to Phil, "I hear you've been making up some beats for *Dance of the Tumblers*."

His face lit up. "Yeah, it's in that section where I have all those rests."

"You want to try it tonight?"

Admittedly, any lover of classical music would have been appalled at what took place that evening, but the audience loved it, and I suspect it may have been the high point in Phil's musical career. The next day Phil came to school and told me now that his grades were coming up his parents were going to try to get the money to put him in a private school. I asked him how he felt about that. He said he didn't want to go because there would be no orchestra.

The last time Margaret, the custodian, caught me working late in my classroom she poked her head in and said, "I guess if you can make one difference in a student's life, that makes all the difference."

While I'll take any difference I can make, that statement has always made me angry. I suspect if all we as teachers could do is make one difference in one student's life, we wouldn't be here. For music educators, the potential for community in the music classroom is an invitation to stretch our work past the students, past the classroom, and into the society we create. And if, indeed, ours is a world of increased isolation, numbness, thanklessness, and such—our work is all the more important and effective. At my spring concert, one of my high school students got up on stage and told the audience, "You have no idea how much Mr. Shieh has put up with and how much he has done for us."

We as music educators have the privilege and pleasure of making change, and we do so with a community that has seen that change and answers its challenge.

—Eric Sheih

Decoding

This year has been a rough year. Although I teach in a middle class suburb, I've had two students die tragic deaths this year. One was murdered, and the other was the victim of an accident. The budget in my district is tight, which makes the tension level at school high. In the past two years, my closest collegial friends have all left my district. Yet each morning I still enjoy coming to work.

There is something difficult to explain about being an elementary music teacher. It's funny how music teachers come to be; unlike most other majors in the education field, music teachers develop out of two loves. We love music, and we love students. It always surprises me when I talk to another teacher and I realize that most didn't become teachers because they really love spelling or math or their specialty. They all teach because of children. If they have a day when their students aren't enchanting, they become discouraged. I'm allowed a more selfish venue. I love children, and I love music. On a bad day at work for one, I have the other. This is the career that encompasses both.

Each day I walk into work, my students love me, no matter how frustrated and annoyed I am with the rest of the world. They make me smile with their joy in living. Sometimes, though, they can be the cause of my stress.

In my first year of teaching, I had a second grade student I was convinced was trying to drive me crazy. She was full of boundless energy, and it always seemed to come out in the middle of my lessons. She had fiery red hair, and her disposition seemed to be just as fiery. She never sat still during my lessons. Sometimes she even got up and ran around the room in the middle of an activity. She bothered other children. She was never on task. She didn't show up for performances. In short, she seemed to go out of her way to do anything but what I was teaching.

I see my students twice a week for twenty-five minutes, which ordinarily is not long enough for any student to do anything disruptive enough to try my patience. I usually have endless patience with children. But this girl made me want to pull my hair out. On most days, I would have her in my classroom for recess because I was trying to adjust her behavior. I had endless conferences with her teachers. They commiserated with me and told me that they had the same problems in their classes and little insight to offer. I tried calling home. Nothing seemed to work.

After two years of this behavior, it just became part of my routine. It was almost part of my lesson plans; I would predict which part of my third grade plan would leave me exasperated with this child.

At the end of her third grade year, I tried a new lesson. As a part of a unit on the Underground Railroad, I posted symbols used by slaves around the building. I taught the children some code songs used by slaves. They had to take a worksheet around the building with them. As they discovered a symbol near a room, they were to knock on the door and sing the code song to the person who answered the door. This way, if they didn't know what the symbol meant, they'd find out by the reaction of that person. Some symbols were good, and the students would get a small prize (a snack), and some were bad (they would lose their recess). The students spent one recess going around the building decoding the symbols.

The lesson was amazingly useful. The students felt some anxiety about picking the wrong symbol and carefully spread the word to each other about what each symbol meant. Very few children knocked on the door of the "bad" symbols. As they worked, the children passed messages in a coded way so that I wouldn't know (or so they thought) that they were telling each other which doors to knock on. Also, they felt some anxiety about knocking on each door, giving them just the slightest insight into what the slaves felt when they were knocking on doors in the middle of the night. However, it was a very difficult lesson to monitor. There were students everywhere, and I was trying to keep them from dropping their trash on the floor, misbehaving, or running in the hallway. At the end of the ten minutes, I was exhausted.

I was so overwhelmed that I wasn't sure if the lesson was worth all that exhaustion. My principal liked it because she saw active learning, and she enjoyed being a part of it (she awarded prizes at her office door for children willing to take the chance of knocking on the principal's door). Other teachers weren't so sure about it because it seemed too chaotic to them. My mind wasn't made up until the end of that day.

As I was walking out to bus duty that afternoon, a fiery redhead followed me. She snuck up behind me and gave me a big hug. She said, "Ms. White, that was an excellent lesson plan. I really enjoyed learning today." I was a little flabbergasted; the words she used hardly sounded like those of a child, especially one who had given me so much frustration in my career.

From that day forward, I never had a problem with her behavior again. In fact, she became one of my model students, taking the lead in activities, and frequently giving up her recesses for a new purpose: to spend time learning more music. This year is her fifth grade year, and finally everyone else is seeing the wonderful girl I see as well. She was awarded a "turn-around" award this year and was a soloist at our big all-district chorus concert.

I'm hooked. Since then, I regularly discover other students like her; students who make me work hard for my money but are definitely worth it. I've always liked a challenge, and it is easy to enjoy coming to work each day when I have some puzzles to solve: What will I do today that will engage a student I didn't expect to be engaged? Which of my students is hiding a musical ability I don't know about? Who is happier to see me every day than I know? And every day, my students don't fail me. I can always look forward to something.

—Regina White Herring

A Supportive Community and Administration

Far too often we hear stories about the trials and tribulations of beginning music teachers regarding the daily struggles they face on multiple fronts. I am friendly with a number of music educators who are outstanding teachers, but are unable to achieve their professional goals. From exchanging war stories with my colleagues, I've found that the obstacles usually come from areas other than their personal teaching abilities or musicianship. The potential problem areas include school administration, parents, and the community at large.

A couple of years ago, while preparing to enter the music education profession, I became nervous, scared, and discouraged with the prospect of having my dreams and goals dashed by unsupportive adults who either don't understand what quality music education is or, even worse, don't believe it is an important enough discipline to be concerned with. I was never worried about the students because I tend to get along pretty well with high school students, and as far as my teaching abilities are concerned, I have plenty of resources to rely on and people to call for help. My deepest and darkest fears lay with the three areas mentioned above, which, to some extent, seemed like they were uncontrollable factors. I heard so many negative stories that I soon came to believe that being a music educator meant taking on a lifetime of battles with us teachers being the martyrs for our causes. I geared up for battle and started applying for jobs.

However, there are jobs where the administration, parents, and community work collaboratively with the music teachers to create some wonderful music education opportunities for the students. I am currently in my second year as a high school band director. At the time I was hired, the high school had a student population of about 1,100 students, and the high school band program had about 110 members. These 110 members were split by skill level into three bands: the concert band, the symphonic band, and the wind ensemble. There was no marching band, and the jazz program consisted of the "stage band," a non-auditioned group that met one night a week for a couple hours. The instrumentation of the program was less than desirable. The communication between the middle school and high school directors was minimal, leading to a significant drop rate between eighth and ninth grades. Upon being hired, I made a list of goals for the program that I wanted to achieve within my first five years, including:

- Starting proper recruitment in the elementary levels to ensure diverse instrumentation in the future.
- Increasing communication between the middle and high school programs and holding eighth grade recruitment activities.
- Beginning a cocurricular (after school only) marching band that would perform at all football games, a few competitions, and a televised parade.
- Beginning an auditioned jazz ensemble that would perform throughout the community and at local and regional festivals or adjudications.
- Realigning the curricular program so that the concert band became the "ninth grade band" and only the symphonic band and wind ensemble members were placed by audition, getting rid of the negative stigma attached with being in the concert band if you are an upper classman.
- Adding into the program of studies/curriculum the requirement that all students meet with the band director during the school day individually for a short lesson or assessment on a regular basis.
- Beginning to travel with the ensembles to sites and performances that have deep significance and educational value.
- Increasing the percentage of students taking private lessons.
- Increasing enrollment in the high school band program to the point where a second high school band director would be necessary.
- Increasing the number of students involved in district, regional, and all-state band.
- Creating a comprehensive Band Parents Association (boosters) with an executive board, monthly meetings, and tax-exempt status as a not-for-profit organization.
- Bringing in guest clinicians/artists/composers.
- Securing a budget that would allow all of these goals to take place.

My first and most important goal is and always will be bettering myself as a teacher and musician so that I may continue to deepen my students' experiences and level of musicianship. This, however, is something that would have been a goal no matter in what district I was teaching. The above list is specific to the school where I teach and the problems/deficiencies I noticed in the program.

When I initially wrote this list, I posted it on my office wall with great enthusiasm and looked forward to, over the years, checking off each one as it was achieved. To my absolute shock and greatest pleasure, in only my second year I can honestly say that all of the above have already been checked off. We now have more than 500 students enrolled in the elementary school band program with a diverse instrumentation. The high school curricular band program has grown to 215, and an additional director is being hired for the coming school year. The marching band has 120 students, and the auditioned jazz band received all 1s and superior ratings. Recruitment activities between the middle and high schools take place, and for the past two years we have had a 99% and 96% retention rate respectively from eighth to ninth grade. The school board approved a new program of studies that includes individual lessons/assessments with the band director during the school day. Our Band Parents Association is now a 503c non-profit organization with a $20,000 budget. The list goes on to include all the goals listed above and more.

When telling colleagues about these accomplishments, they often ask me how I achieved so much in such a short time. What I tell them is that I didn't achieve anything. I simply made our community and district aware of what could be and what still can be. It was the community, students, parents, and administration that made all of this happen so fast. Financially, the administration threw everything they had at the program. The community attended all of our Band Parents Association fund-raisers, and our concerts were packed. The students made the time commitments necessary to expanding the program and cocurricular ensembles. The directors of curriculum, the superintendent, and building administration allowed the band directors' teaching schedules to be conducive to offering individualized assessment. In fall 2005, we moved into a new high school with a state-of-the-art music facility and performing arts center. Because of the move into the new building (the current high school is becoming an additional middle school), all new instruments are being bought. This is all happening in a budget crisis year where the superintendent had to cut $2 million from the budget.

I write this story not to brag. In fact, I feel somewhat awkward telling this story for fear that people may think I am too sure of myself. That couldn't be further from the truth. I write this story to offer some sort of balance to all the disastrous stories we hear about programs being cut, administrators not being supportive, parents giving directors a hard time, and communities being apathetic. I am the first to admit that I am, in many ways, simply lucky that I landed in a place where the arts are ingrained in the culture of the school district and community. These places do exist. They are not easy to find, but they are out there! It is not hopeless! I have a very long way to go in my development as a teacher, but I feel like half the battle is won, and I never had to fight.

—Adam Warshafsky

Because It's Fun!

The very last activity I have students do at the end of the school year is complete a survey. I ask them questions that they answer with varying degrees of seriousness, and their answers give me insight into what it's like to be in my class. When I ask kids why they're taking band next year, the most common answer is "because it's fun!" Even though I leave plenty of space for them to express themselves in detail, very rarely does anyone write more. For many of my middle school students, fun says it all. When I considered the question "What keeps music teachers going?" my immediate response was also "because it's fun!" Although saying so makes me feel a lot like one of my students, it's true. Overwhelmingly, this is why they're in band, and, as it turns out, it's why I'm in band too.

Had I answered this question last year, fun wouldn't have factored into my response for the simple reason that teaching was often overwhelming and rarely enjoyable. I would have said that teaching was my calling; that and my belief that the next year would be better (and it's counterpart assumption that the first year wasn't going to get any worse) kept me going throughout the school year along with the strong support given to me by my family and friends. I still believe that teaching is my calling and that each year will improve as I learn more, and I haven't stopped relying on encouragement from others. But now the reason I regularly get up before sunrise to spend each day with the generally dreaded "middle school student" is simpler still: teaching is routinely (but unpredictably) fun.

Fun comes in many forms. At a most basic level, it's in the day-to-day silliness in class that my students understand is the counterpoint to concentration. I've done impersonations, told embarrassing stories, and created ridiculous similes to help illustrate a musical point, and they reciprocate with stories of their own that make me smile. On a deeper level though, being a music teacher is fun because of the high degree of creativity and autonomy that is present in the job. What I teach, how I teach, and when I teach it are all my own decisions. My principal isn't going to send me an e-mail of the day's lesson plans, and no one has yet demanded that I have something on a desk by 5:00 p.m. on Friday. While this freedom can occasionally be daunting, I enjoy having the space to try new ideas and approaches, and to adapt plans to each class.

This flexibility keeps teaching from being boring—each day is different. I may teach the same concept, but the way I teach it changes in anticipation of or in response to each group of students and the individuals in that group. Approval and appreciation for what I do also make teaching fun. I love concerts for the opportunity to perform, to demonstrate what the students have learned, and for the mainly positive comments from parents and administrators alike.

My students also let me know that they appreciate my efforts. While middle school students may not be known for being fountains of gratitude, when they express appreciation, it is sincere. Perhaps most important, I genuinely like my students and have a good rapport with most of them, which means I take pride in their accomplishments and care about their learning. There were times this year when I couldn't wait for Monday morning because I was looking forward to introducing them to something new. Their expressions of surprise when they do something difficult right for the first time and their pride in what they've learned individually and as a band continually inspire me to challenge them and see how much they can learn. I hope that throughout their lives they'll develop a strong emotional connection to music, so hearing their progress is the most fun of all, because I know that with each new piece of knowledge, they develop a deeper understanding and appreciation for music and music making.

Fun, however, does not mean easy. Teaching middle school band was never easy last year, and there were plenty of times when I was frustrated with any number of the many aspects of my job, including administrative concerns, classroom management, and the pace of student learning. I have no doubt that the future holds a great deal of annoyance, irritation, and stress. In these times the memory or anticipation of success motivates me, and my family and friends give me perspective on my temporary problems. I'm also helped by the advice my mom gave me when I first began teaching: give yourself permission to fail. No one does everything right, and keeping realistic expectations has allowed me to enjoy my successes without feeling terrible about most of my failures.

One of my mentors has now been teaching for thirty-four years. He considers a playful nature to be an essential part of teaching, and he enjoys being a middle school band director so much that he can't think of what he'd rather be doing. He's not about to retire. Although I'm at the other end of my career, I had similar choices. On some days when class is dragging and learning seems slow, I tell my students and remind myself that I didn't become a teacher to be bored. "Let's go!" I want to tell them. "There's so much to learn to play, and you won't believe how much fun it is."

—Stephanie E. Perry

About the Authors

Colleen M. Conway is associate professor of music education at the University of Michigan. Her scholarly interests include instrumental music education, preservice music teacher education, qualitative research, and the mentoring and induction of beginning music teachers. Conway has published more than forty articles on these topics in music education journals, including *Journal of Research in Music Education* and *Bulletin of the Council for Research in Music Education*. She has presented at national and international conferences, including MENC, the Midwest Clinic, AERA, and ISME. Conway is currently on the editorial boards of *UPDATE: Applications of Research in Music Education* and the *Bulletin of the Council for Research in Music Education*. She is program chair of the Research on Induction Special Interest Group of the American Educational Research Association. Her book *Great Beginnings for Music Teachers: A Guide to Mentoring and Induction* was released by MENC in 2003.

Thomas M. Hodgman is associate professor of music at Adrian College, where he is chairman of the music department and director of the choral ensembles. He also is artistic director and principal conductor for the Lenawee Community chorus and is the chorus master of Opera!Lenawee. In addition to his teaching, Hodgman is the North Central Division representative for the College Music Educator's National Conference. He is the executive director for the Adrian Community Music Program at Adrian College and holds graduate degrees in choral conducting from Westminster Choir College and the Eastman School of Music. Prior to his position at Adrian College, Hodgman was director of choral activities at New Jersey University and at Nazareth College in Rochester, New York.